CONTENTS

Alex Gordon
Author

Gerda Gordon
Co-ordinator

Publisher **Ken Laird**
Lang Syne Publishers Ltd.
79 Main Street,
Newtongrange,
Midlothian EH22 4NA
Tel: 0131 344 0414
E Fax: 0845 075 6085
E-mail: info@lang-syne.co.uk
www.langsyneshop.co.uk

Design **Dorothy Meikle**

Pictures
SNS
Vagelis Georgogarion

Print **Printwell Ltd**

LangSyne
PUBLISHING
WRITING *to* REMEMBER

THREE AND EASY...hat-trick hero Scott Sinclair runs away in celebration after completing his terrific threesome against Hearts at Tynecastle on April 2, 2017. Celtic triumphed 5-0 to clinch their sixth successive Premiership title with eight games still to play.

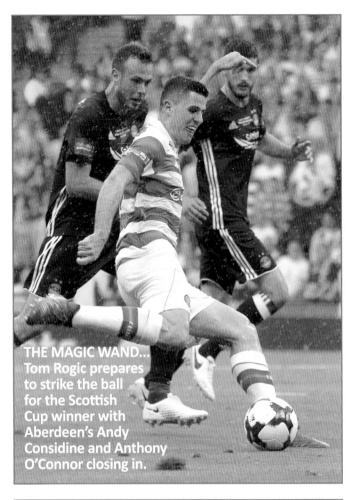

THE MAGIC WAND... Tom Rogic prepares to strike the ball for the Scottish Cup winner with Aberdeen's Andy Considine and Anthony O'Connor closing in.

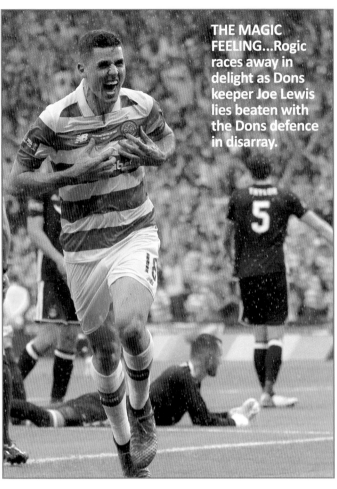

THE MAGIC FEELING...Rogic races away in delight as Dons keeper Joe Lewis lies beaten with the Dons defence in disarray.

TREBLE YELL... the Celtic matchwinner turns in obvious joy – the clean sweep of silverware secured in an incredible campaign.

THE MAN FROM DOWN UNDER...and on top of the world. Rogic can't disguise his happiness as he clutches his shirt.

MINI-HUDDLE... Rogic is congratulated by celebrating team-mates Mikael Lustig and Scott Sinclair.

THE FIST OF GLORY...the Wizard of Oz walks away in triumph after his spectacular solo effort.

THE SPOILS OF WAR...Rogic holds aloft the Scottish Cup, the final piece of the Celtic jigsaw.

SCOTTISH CUP ACTION

WHAT A BELTER...Stuart Armstrong wheels away after thumping in the equaliser against Aberdeen. Kieran Tierney is about to join the celebrations, but Dons winger Jonny Hayes can't disguise his emotions.

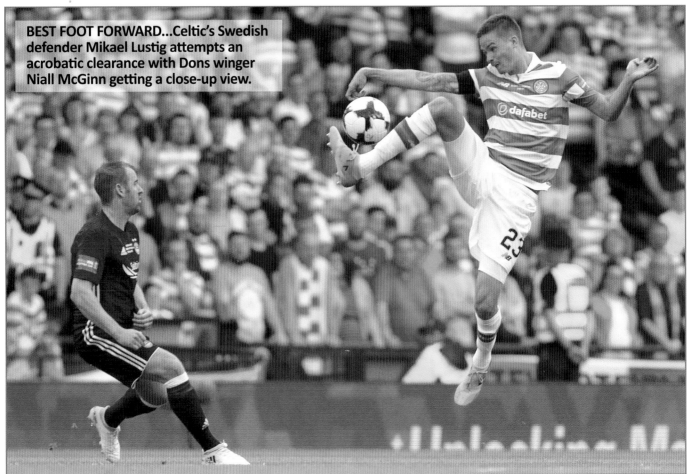

BEST FOOT FORWARD...Celtic's Swedish defender Mikael Lustig attempts an acrobatic clearance with Dons winger Niall McGinn getting a close-up view.

WET, WET, WET...and happy, happy, happy! Brendan Rodgers, drenched and delighted.

THAT SINKING FEELING NUMBER ONE...Scott Sinclair, normally so deadly in front of goal, fires one over the bar as he gets in before defenders Andy Considine and Ash Taylor.

THAT SINKING FEELING NUMBER TWO...the Celtic attacker tries his luck with a left-foot attempt, but Aberdeen keeper Joe Lewis is alert to the danger to block the shot.

OH, NO YOU DON'T...
Aberdeen defender Ash Taylor hauls back Celtic midfielder Stuart Armstrong to earn a booking.

HEAD MASTERS...
Leigh Griffiths and Jonny Hayes duel for the ball.

TENSE TUSSLE...
Callum McGregor and Niall McGinn in a challenge.

SCOTTISH CUP ACTION

WHAT A CHOKER...an emotional Brendan Rodgers with Scott Brown at the final whistle.

PEEK-A-BOO... Leigh Griffiths gets in on the act with Patrick Roberts and Kieran Tierney.

AS EASY AS ONE, TWO, THREE...Leigh Griffiths with the Scottish Cup.

YIPPEE...happy daze for Celtic players Scott Brown, Craig Gordon, Mikael Lustig, Leigh Griffiths, Scott Sinclair, Patrick Roberts and Tom Rogic.

FAN-TASTIC...brave Kieran Tierney celebrates his boyhood idols' win.

FLAMING STAR...Scott Brown has been on fire all season.

Jock Stein *profile*

Unlike many other Celts, I cannot claim that Celtic was my first love... but I can say it will be my last love.

WITH extreme courtesy, Jock Stein stepped aside and pushed open the door of the dressing room to allow the elegantly-dressed individual in the camel-haired coat, smart dark suit and shiny black brogues to make his exit.

Big Jock then made sure the door was shut tight before he turned to the assortment of footballers preparing for kick-off.

With the thumb protruding from a bunched fist, he motioned with his right hand over his shoulder and instructed them: "Right, you can forget everything he has just told you. You don't listen to the likes of him."

The gentleman on the receiving end of the not-so-subtle putdown was Celtic chairman Robert Kelly, who would later be knighted for his services to football.

Broomfield Park, the rundown, ramshackle premises of Airdrie, on a grey Wednesday evening in March 1965, was the unlikely setting for a football legend to be born.

Jock Stein had just taken charge of the Parkhead side, replacing the man who is still the club's all-time leading goalscorer, Jimmy McGrory.

Bertie Auld was stripped and ready for action that spartan evening and recalled: "Jock was immediately telling us all we would do it his way, he was the boss and no-one else.

"Robert Kelly was prone to visiting dressing rooms before games and delivering a sermon to the players. Quite rightly, he did not embrace any unsporting behaviour from anyone wearing green-and-white hoops. 'That's not the Celtic way,' he would stress, time and time again.

"And a lot of the players from that era knew if they got involved in hard, but fair, tackles, and an opponent, God forbid, was injured, there was every chance they would be out of the team for the following match.

"I think Kelly believed it was okay for Celtic players to have lumps kicked out of them and booted all over the park without even an attempt at retaliation.

"The chairman was almost puritanical in the manner he viewed the game. He appeared to want to remove aggression from his players' personality. Yes, we all accepted what he was saying, but we had a job to do for the team and you weren't going to win too many games if you don't have the ball. And you won't get the ball if you don't win your challenges.

"In boxing parlance, it would have been like asking your fighter to go into the ring with one hand tied behind his back. Transfer that philosophy to football and you get the picture.

Sadly, that was often the case back then. And then Big Jock arrived and everything changed in an instant.

"Jimmy McGrory was a lovely man, but he was actually too nice to be a football manager. The players were all well aware he didn't pick the team.

"He would hand in his selection at the board meeting every Thursday night at Parkhead and if the chairman didn't agree with his line-up, he simply changed it.

"Jimmy McGrory would then discover his team for Saturday when it was pinned to the notice board. Remember, this is the Celtic manager we are talking about. ▶

League Table Top Ten

P	Team	Pld	W	D	L	GF	GA	GD	Pts
1	**Celtic**	**34**	**26**	**6**	**2**	**111**	**33**	**78**	**58**
2	Rangers	34	24	7	3	92	31	61	55
3	Clyde	34	20	6	8	64	48	16	46
4	Aberdeen	34	17	8	9	72	38	34	42
5	Hibernian	34	19	4	11	72	49	23	42
6	Dundee	34	16	9	9	74	51	23	41
7	Kilmarnock	34	16	8	10	59	46	13	40
8	Dunfermline Athletic	34	14	10	10	72	52	20	38
9	Dundee United	34	14	9	11	68	62	6	37
10	Motherwell	34	10	11	13	59	60	-1	31

League Cup Final

October 29, 1966: **CELTIC 1** Lennox
RANGERS 0

Simpson; Gemmell, O'Neill; Murdoch, McNeill, Clark; Johnstone, Lennox, McBride, Auld, Hughes (sub: Chalmers).

Scottish Cup Final

April 29, 1967: **CELTIC 2** Wallace (2)
ABERDEEN 0

Simpson; Craig, Gemmell; Murdoch, McNeill, Clark; Johnstone, Wallace, Chalmers, Auld, Lennox.

European Cup Final

May 25, 1967: **CELTIC 2** Gemmell, Chalmers
INTER MILAN 1 Mazzola (pen)

Simpson; Craig, Gemmell; Murdoch, McNeill, Clark; Johnstone, Wallace, Chalmers, Auld, Lennox.

THE CUP THAT CHEERS...Jock Stein proudly holds the European Cup, the pinnacle of his considerable managerial achievements. Celtic became the first British team to conquer Europe when they memorably overcame Inter Milan 2-1 in Lisbon on May 25, 1967.

Celtic, one of the most famous football teams in the world, not some Saturday kick-about mob.

"It was clear from day one, though, Big Jock wouldn't stand for any meddling from the chairman or any of the directors.

"He was the manager of the team and his word was law. You crossed Jock and you paid a heavy price, trust me. I don't think it was purely coincidence we started winning games and trophies again after his arrival."

THE GLORY BHOYS...Jock Stein (extreme left) and manager Jimmy McGrory (second right) with Celtic players Charlie Tully, Bobby Evans, Sean Fallon, Bobby Collins, Bertie Peacock, Neil Mochan and Dick Beattie in the mid-fifties.

Bertie Auld, now a sprightly 79 year old, must have impressed his new boss that frosty, crisp late winter's evening under the dull lights at the home of Airdrie. Celtic trounced their opponents 6-0 and Auld, playing wide on the left wing, struck five of them, two from penalty-kicks. John Hughes claimed the other as Jock Stein signalled his intentions right from the start.

Celtic had often been labelled Scotland's sleeping giant after they had gone without a trophy success since their remarkable 7-1 League Cup triumph over Rangers in season 1957/58. The Ibrox side actually kicked off as favourites that afternoon at Hampden before being humbled by their ancient rivals.

There were many shrewd observers who noted that Celtic were not so much having an extended nap as comatose. Over the miserable, barren years, with Robert Kelly ruling at Parkhead, distinctly-average players were brought in at bargain fees who did nothing to aid the club to strive away from mediocrity. Elastoplast was being utilised when surgery was obviously – and urgently – required.

When it was clear the board would have to do something drastic, they discussed their former player and reserve team coach Jock Stein, who had moved up to management and had been a near-miraculous success at Dunfermline and Hibs. He even piloted the Fife no-hopers to a fairly

sensational 2-0 Scottish Cup Final replay victory over Celtic, of all teams, in 1961.

In late January 1965, Kelly met Stein in secret. Even to this day, it is not clear who instigated the get-together. One train of thought states it was the Celtic chairman, under extreme pressure from frustrated supporters who had taken to staging regular demonstrations after home games. Another belief is that Stein manipulated the confab under the guise of seeking advice from Kelly.

Big Jock had already befriended some well-appointed reporters in the national press. One newspaper leaked the story Wolves, looking for a replacement manager for the departing Stan Cullis, had taken notice of what Stein had achieved at Dunfermline and what he was continuing to contribute at Hibs.

It's not a stretch of the imagination, therefore, to believe Stein arranged the tete-a-tete with Kelly. There can be no doubt the team of his choice to manage would have been Celtic. The link with Wolves could have been merely camouflage. A newsman would have been happy to put his name on that story; Stein could prove to be a powerful ally in years ahead.

Remember, please, Bertie Auld, a shrewd cookie in his own right, always insisted the foxes took to the hills when Stein was in town.

The all-powerful Parkhead decision-maker would have to move swiftly if he harboured any thoughts of asking Stein to return to the east end of Glasgow. A shift to England could very well have seen the manager come off the radar for all time.

What was said that day is open to conjecture. One thing is certain, within another couple of days, Kelly met Stein again. This time he had a very important proposal to put to Big Jock. He asked him if he was prepared to become Celtic manager. Stein didn't need too long to deliver an answer. As he would reveal in later life: "Unlike many other Celts, I cannot claim that Celtic was my first love...but I can say it will be my last love."

Both men shook hands there and then. However, the verbal agreement almost came to nought before the final syllable when the Celtic chairman put it to a strong-willed man he would have Sean Fallon as a joint manager. The Irishman had been McGrory's assistant and, in truth, did most of the training with the players while the manager stayed in his office at the ground and, incredibly enough, sorted out the wages for staff as well as other menial tasks. It is also believed Fallon had been promised the main job when McGrory eventually stepped down.

Jock Stein, forcibly, rejected the offer to share the managerial duties with anyone else. He was very much his own man. Kelly, known to all as a stubborn individual, had to back-track. Stein got his own way; it wouldn't be the last

THREE WISE MEN...Jock Stein is flanked by his trusted backroom staff of coach Neil Mochan (left) and assistant boss Sean Fallon as they discuss the way ahead for Celtic. The trio were all team-mates at the club in the fifties.

BHOYS

CELTIC claimed the Scottish Cup with a 2-0 win over Aberdeen at Hampden where Willie Wallace hit both goals. They played six games in all, including a semi-final replay against Clyde. They scored twenty goals and conceded three.

ZONE

time, either. As a compromise, Fallon remained in his No.2 position.

Stein, though, admitted to close friends he was "embarrassed" at the prospect of walking out on Hibs; he had only taken over at Easter Road from Dunfermline in March the previous year. The Edinburgh team, going well in the league and the Scottish Cup, understandably wished to hold onto their ambitious young manager, who was only forty-one at the time, until the end of the season.

The perceptive Stein agreed to remain in place until the club appointed a new manager. He then manoeuvred a situation that enticed Bob Shankly, brother of Liverpool's legendary gaffer Bill, to leave Dundee and replace him at Hibs early in March.

For all the wrong reasons, Stein's appointment created quite a stir, mainly in the blinkered parts of the west of Scotland. One national newspaper's front page banner headline screeched: STEIN FIRST PROTESTANT MANAGER OF CELTIC.

At least, it didn't shilly-shally with the facts. History had been made at a club which had been formed seventy-seven years earlier by a Marist priest, Brother Walfrid, and had been managed by a succession of Roman Catholics; Willie Maley, who took charge of first team matters for almost forty-three years before being replaced by Jimmy McStay in 1940. Jimmy McGrory became the third Celtic team boss five years later.

Stein's take on the so-called controversy was interesting. "Ach, what are they worried about?" he smiled. "Only twenty-five per cent of Celtic managers have been Protestant."

By Stein's own admission his family weren't "Orange, but they were staunch." Stein was brought up in Burnbank, Lanarkshire, and his father, George, was a fervent Rangers supporter. The family hoped Jock, a useful centre-half or left-half, would one day sign for the Ibrox side. That was the wish of his father. His son should play in the blue-red-and-white of Junior side Blantyre Vics before swapping it for the blue-red-and-white of Rangers.

Jock, though, displayed an exceptional independent streak early in life. He was not rebellious and never displayed the slightest bit of curiosity concerning the religious divides of a small mining community, but, later in life, Stein never made even the remotest attempt to disguise the fact he thoroughly enjoyed beating Rangers.

I interviewed Bertie Auld at length for a book I was writing, 'Celtic: The Awakening', which was published in 2013, and the former midfield craftsman, with his customary forthrightness, told me: "Publicly, Big Jock would inform everyone that a meeting with Rangers was just another

THE BEGINNING...Jock Stein is watched by manager Jimmy McGrory as he signs from Llanelli Town in 1951. He would replace McGrory 14 years later.

game. Privately, the players all knew just how much he enjoyed putting one over our old rivals. I would go as far as to say he detested Rangers. I don't think that is too strong a word. He really disliked them.

"We all knew his background, we realised where his roots lay, but we also saw him after a win over Rangers. You would have needed plastic surgery to get the smile off his face. We could beat any other team 2-0, 3-0, 4-0, you name it and we could still get a rollicking when we turned up for training on Monday.

"If he had seen something that upset him, irrespective of the winning margin, he would give us pelters. However, we could play awful, get a lucky goal and beat Rangers and we never heard a thing; not a murmur. Lose, though, and life wasn't worth living.

"He rarely, if ever, talked about the sectarian divide. He was a Protestant managing a club with Catholic origins and he had Protestant players such as Ronnie Simpson, Willie Wallace, Tommy Gemmell and myself playing for him. Religion didn't come into it as far as he and Celtic were concerned.

"It did across the Clyde, though. For long enough Rangers would not sign a Catholic. It was well-known that they were put off signing a young player who would go on to become world class because of his name, Danny McGrain. If only they had known.

"Jock used to insist if there were two players of equal ability and one was a Catholic and one was a Protestant, he would sign the latter. He would say: 'Well, Rangers can't sign the Catholic, can they?' Sadly, that was the case back then. Jock found it extremely distasteful.

"In truth, though, he was only interested in a guy's playing ability and not the school he had gone to. Maybe that fired him up just that little bit more for games against Rangers."

Back in March, 1965, though, all that was in front of the manager. And so it was that Jock Stein found himself in the antiquated and very public dug-out at age-battered Broomfield on March 10 1965 to take charge of Celtic for the first time.

Extraordinarily, seven of Stein's debut selection went on to win the European Cup just over two years later – Tommy Gemmell, Bobby Murdoch, Billy McNeill, John Clark, Stevie Chalmers, Bobby Lennox and, of course, Auld.

If anyone had made the preposterous prediction on that damp night in darkest Lanarkshire that Celtic would become the first British club to conquer Europe, they would have been more pitied than laughed at.

The Celtic revival was on. The first silverware treble in the club's history wasn't too far away. ∎

TWO OF A KIND...Jock Stein and chairman Robert Kelly could be stubborn, but they had Celtic at heart.

A MAN AND HIS TROPHIES...Jock Stein proudly poses with some of the silverware collection at Parkhead.

Six of the Best

CELTIC 2
RANGERS 0
(September 17, 1966)

CELTIC, who had beaten their ancient rivals 4-0 in a Glasgow Cup-tie at Ibrox the previous month, were warned of a backlash from a team who had splashed £100,000 – a remarkable sum of money at the time – on two players to emphasise their ambitions for a new season.

Dave Smith, a skilful left-sided midfielder, arrived from Aberdeen in a £50,000 deal and old-fashioned inside-forward Alex Smith, no relation, was purchased for an identical fee from Dunfermline. They were both ready for their Old Firm league debut.

It was one they were unlikely to forget. Within four minutes, Jock Stein's men were two goals ahead and the contest was as good as over.

The 70,000 fans were still settling into Parkhead when Celtic scored a quickfire opening goal. John Hughes pushed the ball to Bobby Lennox whose breathtaking acceleration took him past a couple of challenges before he flashed a cross into the penalty area. Joe McBride swung

at the ball and missed completely, but Bertie Auld, following up, made perfect contact and keeper Billy Ritchie was motionless as the midfielder's effort ricocheted into the net off the base of the upright.

Referee Tiny Wharton's watch had just nudged beyond the third minute when the home side were awarded a free-kick following a foul by Jimmy Millar on McBride twenty-five yards out.

Lennox touched it sideways to the masterful Bobby Murdoch who thundered a first-time shot at goal. It rebounded from the Rangers defensive wall back to the midfielder. This time he checked his stride and nonchalantly lofted the ball towards Ritchie's top left-hand corner. The frantic custodian pawed fresh air as the effort unerringly zeroed in on its target.

Celtic's superiority shone through as they strode through the following eighty-six minutes. It was only the second league game of the 1966/67 campaign, but Jock Stein's men had already put down their marker.

Simpson; Gemmell, O'Neill; Murdoch, McNeill, Clark; Johnstone, Lennox, McBride, Auld and Hughes.

A CAPTAIN'S ROLE...Billy McNeill makes a spectacular clearance to thwart Rangers midfielder Alex MacDonald.

THAT OLD FAMILIAR FEELING...
Bobby Murdoch, Bobby Lennox,
Tommy Gemmell and Bertie Auld
celebrate another goal.

HIBS 3
CELTIC 5
(October 8, 1966)

THE Easter Road encounter was one of the most electrifying and entertaining of an unforgettable campaign, splendidly slugged out by two fierce and gifted combatants in front of a spellbound audience of 43,256.

Celtic had just returned to a heroes' welcome after overwhelming FC Zurich 3-0 in the second leg of their European Cup first round confrontation in Switzerland. With the team winning 2-0 in the first game in the east end of Glasgow, it represented a handsome five-goal winning margin.

The travelling fans arrived in fine voice, but they were rendered silent in the tenth minute when Peter Cormack gave the Edinburgh side the lead following Celtic's inability to deal with a straightforward corner-kick. Five minutes later, parity was restored when Joe McBride zipped one low past valiant keeper Thomson Allan at his far post.

On the half-hour mark, McBride again left Allan helpless, but on this occasion the ball clattered off the woodwork. However, before the Hibs defenders could breathe a sigh of relief, Stevie Chalmers emerged to ram home the rebound. But it was all-square again a mere seven minutes later when Billy McNeill was adjudged to have brought down flying winger Eric Stevenson in the box. Left-back Joe Davis made an excellent job of the penalty-kick.

Remarkably, McBride, an alert and lively predator, scored twice before the interval to swing the advantage back in favour of Jock Stein's team. He was a centre-forward who insisted: "When I see the whites of the goalposts, you can be absolutely sure I'll always have a go." He lived up to his maxim on this occasion, as goalie Allan would surely testify. Just to make sure, the marauding McBride netted his fourth and Celtic's fifth goal in the seventy-fourth minute.

Allan McGraw hit a third in the fading moments for a gallant Hibs side, but the points were heading back to Glasgow after another stirring performance from a team who knew the route to goal – and had the players to punish opposing rearguards.

Simpson; Gemmell, O'Neill; Murdoch, McNeill, Clark; Johnstone, McBride, Chalmers, Auld and Hughes.

▶

LORD OF THE WING...Jimmy Johnstone could terrorise any defence.

entrancing football that defied the elements, the Fifers were leading 4-2 and the visitors and reigning champions appeared on the verge of capitulation.

Celtic had walloped their opponents 9-4 on aggregate in their two-legged League Cup quarter-final earlier in the season and their foes clearly sought revenge. And it looked as though they were about to enjoy the privilege of becoming the first team to derail the Jock Stein juggernaut. Ronnie Simpson was beaten twice in the space of three first-half minutes by Hugh Robertson and Pat Delaney.

Bobby Murdoch responded immediately, but Bert Paton restored his side's two-goal lead seven minutes from the turnaround. However, Jimmy Johnstone pulled one back when he pounced on a rebound from keeper Eric Martin.

The 22,000 crowd enjoyed the welcome half-time respite before the hectic action restarted. Within three minutes, the home side were two goals to the good again when Alex Ferguson blasted past Simpson. And that's the way it stood until the sixty-second minute. Bertie Auld, a performer who would never become famous for accepting second best, slid a third beyond Martin and the fight was now on for at least a point.

Celtic lay siege to the Fifers' goal and, seven minutes after Auld's effort, Joe McBride powered his way through the treacherous underfoot conditions before shelling an unstoppable drive high over the shoulder of Martin into the back of the net. Would the champions settle for a hard-earned draw? Not this team.

Centre-half Roy Barry blatantly punched away a crossball in the fading moments and a penalty-kick was awarded. Up stepped McBride and, without the trace of nerves, banged in the winner.

Simpson; Gemmell, O'Neill; Murdoch, McNeill, Clark; Johnstone, Chalmers, McBride, Auld and Lennox.

DUNFERMLINE 4
CELTIC 5
(November 19, 1966)

CELTIC were on the brink of their first domestic defeat of the season until they produced the most amazing and courageous comeback of a memorable campaign.

East End Park was a mudheap on a rain-lashed afternoon and it looked as though the Parkhead side's hopes of survival were disappearing in the swamp. After just over an hour of

CELTIC 6
PARTICK THISTLE 2
(December 17, 1966)

ALL eyes were on Willie Wallace, the club's £30,000 signing from Hearts eleven days earlier, as he lined up to make his debut against the men from Maryhill.

The stocky raider – only Jock Stein's second signing for the club following his £22,000 purchase of Joe McBride in June 1965 – lined up in an adventurous forward line that simply guaranteed goals. McBride led the attack that crisp afternoon, on a frost-covered playing surface, with Wallace and Stevie Chalmers beside him and Bobby Lennox as back-up.

It took the new signing a mere two minutes before he scored the first of his 135 goals in the green-and-white hoops. Bertie Auld sprung a surprise on the Firhill outfit by abandoning his role on the left to race down the right wing before delivering a peach of a cross into the danger zone. McBride knocked the ball across the face of goal and Wallace headed into the inviting net from six yards.

Chalmers claimed a second in the fourteenth minute following a corner-kick and the 25,000 audience had more to cheer shortly afterwards when Wallace rattled in No.3. Bobby Murdoch hammered in the fourth before Arthur Duncan pulled one back before the interval.

Winter's chill was accompanied by swirling rain and an angry wind at the restart, but it failed to knock the Celtic players out of their stride. McBride, after only eight minutes, netted the fifth – his thirty-sixth strike in a campaign that would be wrecked by injury later in the month. Tommy Gibb, an elegant left-sided midfielder, scorched in a second for Thistle, but, once again, the champions discovered the perfect reply with a sixth and final goal from Chalmers fifteen minutes from time.

The speedy attacker, due to celebrate his thirty-first birthday on Boxing Day, was thought to be the likely candidate to drop out to make way for the incoming Wallace, who, at that time, was the most expensive acquistion in Celtic's history. It was clear Stein hadn't paid top dollar for the versatile performer to occupy a seat in the stand.

Chalmers had been at the club almost eight years since arriving from Shettleston Juniors in February 1959 and wasn't keen to step aside for anyone. On May 25, 1967, he would score Celtic's most famous goal.

A TOTAL of twenty-one players were used during the season. In all five competitions won by the club, they scored 196 goals in sixty-two games. They won 51 and drew eight.

Simpson;
Gemmell,
O'Neill;
Murdoch,
McNeill,
Clark;
Chalmers,
Wallace,
McBride,
Lennox and Auld.

DANGERMAN...Bobby Lennox was a penalty box predator, always on the look-out for an opening. On this occasion, he is thwarted by Hearts keeper Jim Cruickshank.

CELTIC 5 DUNDEE 1
(January 7, 1967)

THIS was a crucial triumph in a season when winning had become a welcome habit. Celtic had carelessly surrendered their unbeaten record in an untypically poor performance against Dundee United at Tannadice on Hogmanay.

Jock Stein's men were leading 2-1 through strikes from Bobby Lennox and Willie Wallace with seventeen minutes left to play on Tayside when the roof caved in on them. Dennis Gillespie launched a long-range drive high past Ronnie Simpson for the equaliser and, remarkably, only two minutes later, the home side took the lead through Ian Mitchell and held on to earn the distinction of becoming the first team to inflict a league defeat on the champions in nine months.

So, after the games against Rangers and Clyde had been frozen off in Arctic Scotland as a merciless 1967 made its introduction, it was vitally important to witness how the

MASTER OF THE MIDFIELD...
Bobby Murdoch could create mayhem with his passing and shooting. Tommy Callaghan looks on appreciatively.

Celtic players would respond to a shock reversal. A crowd of 37,000 hardy souls turned out on a chilly afternoon to welcome the players to another year laced with hope and expectation. Their concerns were swept away in a gloriously-orchestrated triumph over a strong Dens Park line-up.

A determined Celtic outfit didn't require any assistance from their opponents, but they got it, anyway, when the unfortunate Bobby Wilson diverted a Bobby Murdoch effort beyond his own goalkeeper, John Arrol. Ninety seconds later, Murdoch split the visitors' rearguard with a penetrating pass straight to the feet of Wallace and he blitzed a second into the net. In the twentieth minute, it was Jimmy Johnstone's turn to join the cavalcade as he got on the end of Charlie Gallagher's sweet free-kick.

Gallagher, who for so long performed in the shadow of Bertie Auld, was a gifted midfielder with outstanding poise and he demonstrated that quality in the twenty-eighth minute when he tamed the ball, turned neatly and struck a shot of awesome power and precision. Once more, Arrol had no answer.

After the interval, Kenny Cameron pulled one back, but, with fitting timing, Wallace fired in the fifth and final goal in the last minute to bring down the curtain on the first game of a momentous year for Celtic and the supporters.

Simpson; Craig, Gemmell; Murdoch, McNeill, Clark; Johnstone, Wallace, Chalmers, Gallagher and Lennox.

RANGERS 2
CELTIC 2
(May 6, 1967)

CELTIC were singing in the rain at storm-lashed Ibrox Stadium as they fought all the way for the point they required to retain the Scottish First Division title. Not too many fans in attendance that soaking and eventful afternoon, even the most optimistic among the Parkhead following, could have predicted their favourites would win it on another seven successive seasons.

As raindrops the size of golf balls incessantly pelted Glasgow that day, Celtic were about to make absolutely certain their crown would not be swept away. Jimmy Johnstone, in particular, was in a defiant mood as he skimmed over the quagmire that doubled as a football pitch. Unstoppable Jinky gloried in the Govan glaur, a wondrous sight for the beholders wearing green-and-white favours.

The downpour, with the heavy, menacing clouds bursting over the city early in the morning, created chaos with travel and the crowd was a 'mere' 74,000 when 90,000 fans were anticipated. Jock Stein's champions went into the foray with two clean sheets in the previous Old Firm games that season – the 2-0 victory in the league at Parkhead and the 1-0 triumph in the League Cup Final at Hampden.

However, with only four minutes remaining in the first-half, Rangers broke the barrier and there was little Ronnie Simpson could do to prevent a thunderous 25-yard drive from Sandy Jardine from exploding into his top right-hand corner of the net. Amazingly, Celtic levelled in an instant when Bobby Lennox squeezed an effort under keeper Norrie Martin. The ball struck the post and Johnstone gleefully arrived to thump in the rebound.

In the seventy-fourth minute, the wee wing wizard scored a spectacular solo goal that left team-mates, opponents and supporters gasping with delight and dismay in equal measures. He picked up a right-wing throw-in from Stevie Chalmers midway in the Rangers half. No danger threatened as he ambled forward, with left-back Davie Provan pushing him inside onto his so-called weaker left foot. Jinky picked up momentum as the defender trailed behind him and, without warning, hit a shot of devasating power that rocketed from twenty yards high past the astonished Martin. The ball arrived at its destination with a thud that sent showers of rain water from the rigging spraying in all directions.

Roger Hynd forced in a late equaliser, but it meant little. The championship prize would be extending its stay in the Parkhead trophy cabinet for another year where it later threatened to take up permanent residence.

Simpson; Craig, Gemmell; Murdoch, McNeill, Clark; Johnstone, Wallace, Chalmers, Auld and Lennox. ◼

WELL DONE, MY SON... Jock Stein and Billy McNeill, his skipper, always had a special bond – as it clearly shows in this image after yet another win.

BHOYS

BOBBY LENNOX brought the curtain down on a marvellous season when he netted the winner in the 1-0 triumph over Real Madrid at the Bernabeu Stadium in Alfredo di Stefano's Testimonial Match on June 7.

ZONE

League Results

September 10, 1966:
CLYDE 0
CELTIC 3 Chalmers, McBride, Hughes
Simpson; Gemmell, O'Neill; Murdoch, McNeill, Clark; Chalmers, Lennox, McBride, Auld, Hughes.

September 17: **CELTIC 2** Auld, Murdoch
RANGERS 0
Simpson; Gemmell, O'Neill; Murdoch, McNeill, Clark; Johnstone, Lennox, McBride, Auld, Hughes.

September 24: **DUNDEE 1** Penman
CELTIC 2 Lennox, Chalmers
Simpson; Gemmell, O'Neill; Murdoch, McNeill, Clark; Johnstone, Lennox, McBride (sub: Chalmers), Auld, Hughes.

October 1: **CELTIC 6** Johnstone (2), Lennox (2), McBride (2)
ST JOHNSTONE 1 Kilgannon
Simpson; Gemmell, O'Neill; Murdoch, McNeill, Clark; Johnstone, Lennox, McBride, Auld, Hughes.

October 8: **HIBS 3** Cormack, Davis pen, McGraw
CELTIC 5 McBride 4, Chalmers
Simpson; Gemmell, O'Neill; Murdoch, McNeill, Clark; Johnstone, McBride, Chalmers, Auld, Hughes.

October 15: **CELTIC 3** Lennox (2), McBride
AIRDRIE 0
Simpson; Young, Gemmell; Clark, McNeill, O'Neill; Chalmers, Lennox, McBride, Gallagher, Hughes.

October 24: **CELTIC 5** Lennox, Hughes, Johnstone 2, Gemmell
AYR UNITED 1 Black
Simpson; Gemmell, O'Neill; Murdoch, McNeill, Clark; Johnstone, Lennox, Chalmers, Auld, Hughes.

November 2: **CELTIC 7** Johnstone, McBride (3), Chalmers (2), Auld
STIRLING ALBION 3 McGuinness, Reid, Kerray
Simpson; Gemmell, O'Neill; Murdoch, McNeill, Clark; Johnstone, Gallagher (sub: Craig), McBride, Chalmers, Auld.

November 5: **CELTIC 1** Gemmell
ST MIRREN 1 Treacy
Simpson; Craig, O'Neill; Murdoch, Gemmell, Clark; Johnstone, McBride, Chalmers, Auld, Lennox.

November 12: **FALKIRK 0**
CELTIC 3 McBride (2, 1 pen), Auld
Simpson; Gemmell, O'Neill; Murdoch, McNeill, Clark; Chalmers, Gallagher, McBride, Lennox, Auld.

November 19: **DUNFERMLINE 4** Robertson, Delaney, Paton, Ferguson
CELTIC 5 Murdoch, Johnstone, Auld, McBride (2, 1 pen)
Simpson; Gemmell, O'Neill; Murdoch, McNeill, Clark; Johnstone, Chalmers, McBride, Auld, Lennox.

November 26: **CELTIC 3** Miller og, McBride (2, 1 pen)
HEARTS 0
Simpson; Gemmell, O'Neill; Murdoch, McNeill, Clark; Johnstone, Chalmers, McBride, Lennox, Auld

December 3: **KILMARNOCK 0**
CELTIC 0
Simpson; Gemmell, O'Neill; Murdoch, McNeill, Clark; Johnstone, Chalmers, McBride, Lennox, Auld.

December 10: **CELTIC 4** Chalmers (3), Murdoch
MOTHERWELL 2 Murray, Lindsay
Simpson; Gemmell, O'Neill; Murdoch, McNeill, Clark; Johnstone, Wallace, Chalmers, Lennox, Auld. Sub: Cattenach.

December 17: **CELTIC 6** Wallace (2), Murdoch, Chalmers (2), McBride
PARTICK THISTLE 2 Duncan, Gibb
Simpson: Gemmell; Murdoch, McNeill, Clark; Chalmers, Wallace, McBride, Lennox, Auld.

December 24: **ABERDEEN 1** Melrose
CELTIC 1 Lennox
Simpson; Gemmell, O'Neill; Murdoch, McNeill, Clark; Chalmers, Auld, McBride, Wallace, Lennox.

December 31: **DUNDEE UNITED 3** Dossing, Gillespie, Mitchell
CELTIC 2 Lennox, Wallace
Simpson; Gemmell, O'Neill; Murdoch, McNeill, Clark; Chalmers, Lennox, Wallace, Auld, Hughes.

BHOYS ZONE

TOMMY GEMMELL and John Clark were Celtic's only ever-presents in the triumphant 1966/67 season. They played in all sixty-two games. Captain Billy McNeill missed one – a 1-1 draw with St Mirren at Parkhead on November 5, 1966.

BHOYS ZONE

STEVIE CHALMERS netted Celtic's first league goal of the season when they beat Clyde 3-0 at Shawfield on Saturday, September 10, 1966. He also got the club's last competitive goal of the season with the winner against Inter Milan.

January 7, 1967: CELTIC 5 Wilson (og), Gallagher, Wallace (2), Johnstone
DUNDEE 1 Cameron
Simpson; Craig, Gemmell; Murdoch, McNeill, Clark; Johnstone, Wallace, Chalmers, Gallagher, Lennox.

January 11: CELTIC 5 Chalmers (2), Gallagher, Gemmell, Lennox
CLYDE 1 Gilroy
Simpson; Craig, Gemmell; Murdoch, McNeill, Clark; Johnstone, Wallace, Chalmers, Gallagher, Lennox.

January 14: ST JOHNSTONE 0
CELTIC 4 Johnstone (2), Chalmers, Lennox
Simpson; Craig, Gemmell; Murdoch, McNeill, Clark; Johnstone, Wallace, Chalmers, Auld, Lennox.

January 21: CELTIC 2 Wallace, Chalmers
HIBS 0
Simpson; Craig, Gemmell; Murdoch, McNeill, Clark; Johnstone, Wallace, Chalmers, Auld, Hughes.

February 4: AIRDRIE 0
CELTIC 3 Chalmers, Johnstone, Auld
Simpson; Craig, Gemmell; Murdoch, McNeill, Clark; Johnstone, Wallace, Chalmers, Auld, Hughes.

February 11: AYR UNITED 0
CELTIC 5 Johnstone, Hughes, Chalmers (3)
Simpson; Craig, Gemmell; Murdoch, McNeill, Clark; Johnstone, Wallace, Chalmers, Gallagher, Hughes.

February 25: STIRLING ALBION 1 Peebles
CELTIC 1 Hughes
Simpson; Craig, Gemmell; Murdoch, McNeill, Clark; Johnstone, Wallace, Chalmers, Auld, Hughes.

March 4: ST MIRREN 0
CELTIC 5 Wallace (2), Hughes, Lennox, Gemmell (pen)
Simpson; Craig, Gemmell; Murdoch, McNeill, Clark; Hughes, Gallagher, Wallace, Lennox, Auld.

March 18: CELTIC 3 Chalmers, Wallace, Gemmell (pen)
DUNFERMLINE 2 Ferguson (2)
Simpson; Gemmell, O'Neill; Murdoch, McNeill, Clark; Hughes, Gallagher, Chalmers, Wallace, Lennox.

March 20: CELTIC 5 Chalmers (2), Auld, Hughes, Gemmell (pen)
FALKIRK 0
Simpson; Craig, Gemmell; Murdoch, McNeill, Clark; Johnstone, Wallace, Chalmers, Auld, Hughes.

March 25: HEARTS 0
CELTIC 3 Auld, Wallace, Gemmell (pen)
Simpson; Craig, Gemmell; Murdoch (sub: Lennox), McNeill, Clark; Johnstone, Wallace, Chalmers, Auld, Hughes.

March 27: PARTICK THISTLE 1 Flanagan
CELTIC 4 Lennox, Chalmers 2, Wallace
Simpson; Craig, Gemmell; Wallace, McNeill, Clark; Johnstone, Gallagher, Chalmers, Lennox, Auld.

April 8: MOTHERWELL 0
CELTIC 2 Wallace, Gemmell (pen)
Simpson; Craig, Gemmell; Wallace, McNeill, Clark; Hughes, Lennox, Chalmers, Gallagher (sub: Brogan), Auld.

April 19: ABERDEEN 0
CELTIC 0
Simpson; Craig, Gemmell; Murdoch, McNeill, Clark; Johnstone, Wallace, Chalmers, Auld, Lennox.

May 3: CELTIC 2 Gemmell (pen), Wallace
DUNDEE UNITED 3 Hainey, Gillespie, Graham
Simpson; Craig, Gemmell; Murdoch, McNeill, Clark; Johnstone, Gallagher, Wallace, Lennox, Hughes.

May 6: RANGERS 2 Jardine, Hynd
CELTIC 2 Johnstone (2)
Simpson; Craig, Gemmell; Murdoch, McNeill, Clark; Johnstone, Wallace, Chalmers, Auld, Lennox.

May 15: CELTIC 2 Lennox, Wallace
KILMARNOCK 0
Fallon; Craig, Gemmell; Murdoch, Cushley, Clark; Johnstone, McNeill, Wallace, Auld, Lennox.

THREE goalkeepers turned out for Celtic throughout the season – Ronnie Simpson (60 appearances), John Fallon (1) and Bent Martin (1).

Incisive and Lethal

CELTIC 1
RANGERS 0
(October 29, 1966)

THE goal that won the League Cup – the first trophy in Celtic's triumphant march towards a historic clean sweep of silverware in season 1966/67 – was so typical of a team under the guidance of Jock Stein.

It was swift, incisive and lethal in its gloriously simple execution. The Parkhead men were defending the League Cup they had won during the previous campaign against the same persistent opponents. On that occasion, John Hughes thumped two first-half penalty-kicks beyond Rangers keeper Billy Ritchie to secure an edgy 2-1 victory.

BUZZBOMB...Bobby Lennox was often the scourge of Rangers. Here he celebrates another goal against the Ibrox side.

Celtic were the bookies' favourites to complete the double over their lifelong nemesis. The Govan outfit were adamant they would get their revenge and manager Scot Symon insisted his side had improved in the intervening twelve months. A crowd of 94,532 was in place by kick-off on a grey, foreboding October afternoon at Hampden, Scottish football's ancient football fortress.

Stein looked to his masterful midfield partnership of Bobby Murdoch and Bertie Auld to take control of proceedings while reminding frontline duo Joe McBride and Bobby Lennox of the importance of quick movement and subtle interchanging to unsettle the Rangers central rearguard. Captain Billy McNeill would be up against the erratic George McLean, a rangy centre-forward who flitted effortlessly between wonderful and woeful in the same ninety minutes.

Full-backs Tommy Gemmell, playing on the right, and Willie O'Neill, on the opposite flank, realised they faced a torrid examination of their defensive skills as they were in direct combat with speed merchants Willie Henderson and Willie Johnson.

So, as the mists rolled over the south side of Glasgow, battle lines were drawn by the time 6ft-plus referee Tom 'Tiny' Wharton blew his whistle bang on three o'clock to get the latest episode of the continuing and always-intriguing Old Firm adventure underway at the national stadium.

The only goal of a grim, resolute encounter arrived in the eighteenth minute and it must be admitted it was an effort worthy of winning any trophy. The lightning raid on the Rangers barricade was carried out with stealth and pace as Stein's men struck at the very heart of their opponents' defensive armour.

Auld, bestowed with the ability to see two moves ahead of the opposition, flighted in a cross to the edge of the penalty area, the ball simply caressed by his left foot. McBride, muscular and brave, outjumped the Ibrox defenders to nod the ball into the path of speedster Lennox.

The player known as Buzzbomb zipped onto the headed pass and, without breaking stride, lashed an unstoppable effort high past the bewildered Norrie Martin into the roof of the net from eight yards. The ball nestled in the rigging before John Greig, Ronnie McKinnon and their defensive cohorts had the chance to blink never mind react.

To be fair, Rangers retaliated with vigour and no little

PYRAMID OF PLEASURE... Lou Macari, Harry Hood and Jimmy Johnstone celebrate a goal.

menace. Gemmell and O'Neill had their work cut out trying to stem the raids on the flanks by the tricky and elusive double-act of Henderson and Johnston and McNeill was coping well with the unorthodox qualities of the enigmatic McLean.

Chances were few and far between for both teams, but Celtic survived a scare with only thirteen minutes to go when Alex Smith, a midfielder thrown up front to accompany McLean as the clock ticked down, managed to squeeze the ball under Ronnie Simpson.

The anxious onlookers held their collective breath as the attempt rolled inexorably towards the line. Would it have enough oomph to see it reach the net? Valiant left-back O'Neill didn't wait for an answer. He covered the ground quickly to catch the ball as it reached the goal-line and, without any attempt at finesse, hammered the sphere to safety.

It hadn't been a spellbinding display by the victors, but elated manager Stein simply stated afterwards: "We came here to win the League Cup and we did that."

No-one at Parkhead realised it at the time, but this Celtic team, its manager and players were on the verge of a very special and extraordinary season in the club's history.

Simpson; Gemmell, O'Neill; Murdoch, McNeill, Clark; Johnstone, Lennox, McBride, Auld and Hughes (sub: Chalmers). ▨

League Cup

Group stages

August 13, 1966: **HEARTS 0**
CELTIC 2 McBride (2, 1 pen)
Simpson; Gemmell, O'Neill; Murdoch, McNeill, Clark; Johnstone, McBride, Chalmers, Lennox, Auld.

August 17: **CELTIC 6** Lennox (2), McBride (3, 1 pen), Chalmers
CLYDE 0
Simpson; Gemmell, O'Neill; Murdoch, McNeill, Clark; Johnstone, McBride, Chalmers, Lennox, Auld.

August 20: **CELTIC 8** Lennox (2), McBride (4, 1 pen), Auld, Chalmers
ST.MIRREN 2 Treacy 2
Simpson; Gemmell, O'Neill; Murdoch, McNeill, Clark; Johnstone, McBride, Chalmers, Lennox, Auld.

August 27: **CELTIC 3** McBride (2, 1 pen), Chalmers
HEARTS 0
Simpson; Gemmell, O'Neill; Murdoch, McNeill, Clark; Johnstone, McBride, Chalmers, Hughes, Auld.

August 31: **CLYDE 1** Gilroy
CELTIC 3 McBride (2, 1 pen), Gemmell
Simpson; Gemmell, O'Neill; Murdoch, McNeill, Clark; Johnstone, McBride, Chalmers, Lennox, Auld.

September 3: **ST MIRREN 0**
CELTIC 1 Murdoch
Simpson; Craig, Gemmell; Murdoch, McNeill, Clark; Johnstone (sub: O'Neill), McBride, Chalmers, Lennox, Gallagher.

September 14: Quarter-finals: 1st leg:
CELTIC 6 McNeill, Johnstone, McBride (pen), Auld (2), Hughes
DUNFERMLINE 3 Ferguson 2, Hunter
Simpson; Gemmell, O'Neill; Murdoch, McNeill, Clark; Johnstone, McBride, Chalmers, Auld, Hughes.

September 21: Quarter-finals: 2nd leg:
DUNFERMLINE 1 Fleming
CELTIC 3 McNeill, Chalmers (2)
Simpson; Gemmell, O'Neill; Murdoch, McNeill, Clark; Johnstone, Chalmers, McBride, Auld, Hughes.

October 17: Semi-final:
CELTIC 2 Murdoch, McBride
AIRDRIE 0
Simpson; Gemmell, O'Neill; Murdoch, McNeill, Clark; Johnstone, McBride, Chalmers, Auld, Lennox.

October 29: Final:
CELTIC 1 Lennox
RANGERS 0
Simpson; Gemmell, O'Neill; Murdoch, McNeill, Clark; Johnstone, Lennox, McBride, Auld, Hughes (sub: Chalmers).

Willie's the Wonder Bhoy!

CELTIC 2
ABERDEEN 0
(April 29, 1967)

WILLIE WALLACE kicked off the season wondering what the future held in store. He was unhappy at his club Hearts and had refused the offer of a new contract. Newcastle United and Stoke City were monitoring his situation and a move across the border looked imminent.

The chunky forward recalled: "I was in dispute with Hearts and just wanted a transfer. English clubs were showing an interest and it looked as though I would be packing my bags.

"Then Jock Stein came on the scene and he didn't have to try too hard to sell Celtic to me. As soon as I realised there was a chance of me going to Celtic Park and working alongside Big Jock, there was no choice to make. Newcastle

United and Stoke City, with all due respect, had no chance of getting my signature on transfer forms when Celtic became an option."

The Parkhead manager made his move for the versatile Wallace after his team had drawn a blank for the first time during the season in a goalless draw against Kilmarnock at Rugby Park on December 3, 1966. Three days later, Stein parted with £30,000 to sign the twenty-six-year-old attacker who had won three full international caps with the Tynecastle club.

However, there was no quickfire debut for Wallace. Stein was far from satisfied with his level of fitness and ordered trainer Neilly Mochan to get him up to the required standard he expected of his Celtic players. Wallace was in the Parkhead stand on December 10 to watch his new team-mates overwhelm Motherwell 4-2 with Stevie Chalmers thumping a hat-trick past Peter McCloy. The following week, Wallace netted two in a 6-2 victory over Partick Thistle and his career in the east end of Glasgow was up and running.

Hollywood, even at its most far-fetched, couldn't have written a more fascinating script for the likeable Wallace. Unfortunately, because of a registration mix-up, he was forced to miss the dramatic and compelling European Cup quarter-final ties against Vojvodina Novi Sad, a team of genuine quality from Yugoslavia. A last-minute trademark headed goal from Billy McNeill propelled Celtic through to the semi-finals of Europe's elite tournament and Wallace made his debut at the highest level against Dukla Prague, the worthy champions of Czechoslovakia. There was no way the

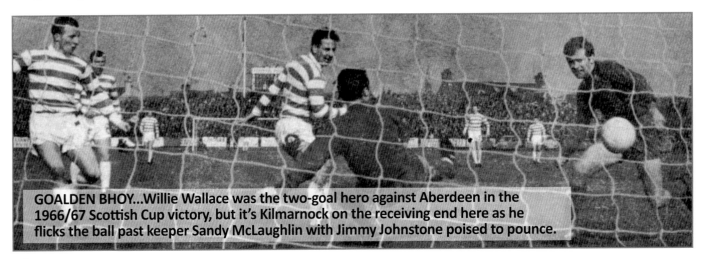

GOALDEN BHOY...Willie Wallace was the two-goal hero against Aberdeen in the 1966/67 Scottish Cup victory, but it's Kilmarnock on the receiving end here as he flicks the ball past keeper Sandy McLaughlin with Jimmy Johnstone poised to pounce.

A BARGAIN...Willie Wallace who cost only £30,000 from Hearts.

Scottish Cup

January 28, 1967: First Round:
CELTIC 4 Murdoch, Gemmell, Auld, Chalmers
ARBROATH 0
Simpson; Craig, Gemmell; Murdoch, McNeill, Clark; Gallagher, Wallace, Chalmers, Auld, Hughes.

February 18: Second Round:
CELTIC 7 Chalmers, Lennox (3), Hughes, Wallace (2)
ELGIN CITY 0
Simpson; Cattenach, Gemmell; Murdoch (sub: Wallace), McNeill, Clark; Johnstone, Lennox, Chalmers, Gallagher, Hughes.

March 11: Third Round:
CELTIC 5 Gemmell (pen), Chalmers, Wallace, Murdoch, Lennox
QUEEN'S PARK 3 Gemmell (og), Hopper (2)
Simpson; Cattenach, Gemmell; Murdoch, McNeill, Clark; Johnstone, Wallace, Chalmers, Auld, Lennox.

April 1: Semi-final:
CELTIC 0
CLYDE 0
Simpson; Craig, Gemmell; Wallace, McNeill, Clark; Johnstone, Auld, Chalmers, Lennox, Hughes.

April 5: Semi-final replay:
CELTIC 2 Lennox, Auld
CLYDE 0
Simpson; Craig, Gemmell; Wallace, McNeill, Clark; Johnstone (sub: Hughes), Gallagher, Chalmers, Auld, Lennox.

April 29: Final:
CELTIC 2 Wallace (2)
ABERDEEN 0
Simpson; Craig, Gemmell; Murdoch, McNeill, Clark; Johnstone, Wallace, Chalmers, Auld, Lennox.

player would take stage fright; this was the platform made for Willie Wallace.

On a still Glasgow evening on April 12, 1967, he thundered in two second-half goals to give Celtic a 3-1 advantage to take to the home of their Czech opponents. Surprisingly, Stein removed his goal threat in the Julaska Stadium and ordered Wallace to shadow Dukla's most accomplished performer, captain and midfielder Jozef Masopust, a former European Footballer of the Year. The Czech's threat was nullified such was the diligence displayed by Wallace in an unusual role and the encounter ended scoreless. Thus, Celtic had a European Cup Final date to look forward to in Lisbon against mighty Inter Milan on May 25, 1967.

Four days after the semi-final stalemate, Wallace was restored to his place in attack as Billy McNeill led out his Celtic team to face Aberdeen in the Scottish Cup Final at Hampden on a bright and sunny afternoon with a remarkable attendance of 126,102 waiting to be entertained. Those of a Parkhead persuasion among the vast numbers were not to be disappointed. Willie Wallace scored two superbly-timed goals – one in each half – and trophy number two, following the League Cup, was heading back across Glasgow after an absence of twelve months.

The first goal arrived three minutes before the interval when Bobby Lennox, with his usual breathtaking burst of electrifying acceleration, latched onto a diagonal pass from Bertie Auld and burst into the Dons penalty area on the left. He hit a pass on the run and Wallace materialised at the near post to nonchalantly sidefoot the ball past the static Bobby Clark, clearly bemused at the speed of the move.

Four minutes after the turnaround, with Celtic swarming all over their crimson-clad opponents, Wallace doubled their advantage. Jimmy Johnstone worked wonder as he chased a long pass to the bye-line that looked to be heading out of

play. However, the little winger managed to twist his body in mid-air and hook a cross into the danger zone. Wallace was ideally positioned to strike the ball on the half-volley and the ball whizzed high past the helpless Bobby Calrk for the killer second goal. They could have bedecked the famous old trophy in green and white ribbons at that precise moment – there was no way back for Aberdeen.

Willie Wallace went up the famous Hampden steps to collect his first Scottish Cup winners' medal. The Peter Pan of goalkeepers, Ronnie Simpson, at thirty-six years of age, was also getting his hands on a badge from the competition for the first time. These were happy times at Celtic. And they were about to get even better.

Simpson; Craig, Gemmell; Murdoch, McNeill, Clark; Johnstone, Wallace, Chalmers, Auld and Lennox. ∎

We Conquer Continent

CELTIC 2
INTER MILAN 1
(May 25, 1967)

THIRTY-ONE seconds. One throw-in. Six passes. A thundering shot. That's all it took for Celtic to turn football on its head on that magical, memorable, exhilarating day in Lisbon on May 25, 1967.

For over an hour the marauding green and white legions had battered away at the Inter Milan goal without success. Goalkeeper Giuliano Sarti had been seen as a possible weak link in the Inter Milan defensive armoury which was otherwise festooned with seasoned internationals. But his was an extraordinary act of defiance that day; an impressive one-man barricade standing in the way of Celtic and destiny. He repelled raid after raid with one of the most astonishing goalkeeping performances ever witnessed.

On the rare occasions when he was beaten, the angels appeared to be on his side. Bertie Auld, sensing a rare opening, clipped the crossbar with a cunning left-foot effort while running at speed. Shots and headers rained down on the black-clad No.1 who dealt with everything with an annoying assurance. Jock Stein ventured to the touchline, his massive left paw pointing the way for his troops. "Keep going," he urged. "Keep moving forward."

Sixty-one minutes. Still Sarti and Inter are standing firm. Sixty-two minutes. Still nothing doing. Sixty-three minutes. Celtic have a shy thirty yards from the goal-line on the left. Willie Wallace, confronted with the giant frame of Giacinto Facchetti, is looking for a team-mate in a good position. Facchetti, blocking his view, holds his ground. Wallace shapes to throw it and changes his mind. Gemmell looms into view to offer an option. The ball duly drops at his right foot. A quick switch across the park to Jim Craig on the right.

Craig rolls it inside for Bobby Murdoch who is crowded out on the edge of the box and the ball is retrieved by Jimmy Johnstone, on the left. He touches it back to John Clark who

IT cost exactly £42,000 to assemble the Lisbon Lions. The only two players who cost transfer fees were Willie Wallace (£30,000 from Hearts) and Bertie Auld (£12,000 from Birmingham City).

thrusts it foward again to Murdoch, this time in the old inside-left channel thirty yards from goal. The Italians, methodical as ever, are refusing to be put off their stride. They regroup, cover, pick up a man, shut down space. Celtic continue to show commendable patience as they pass the ball around.

Murdoch slips a simple pass in front of the galloping Craig. He controls the ball as he gathers momentum heading for the danger zone. Another touch – three in all – before squaring across to Gemmell. There is no break in his stride as he reaches the eighteen-yard box with precision timing before clubbing the ball high past Sarti. The unbeatable is beaten at last. Hallelujah!

Thirty-one seconds. A throw-in. Six passes. One thundering shot. That's all it took.

Liam Brady, who had the distinction of serving both Celtic and Inter Milan, recalled watching the game on television in his native Dublin. "Inter actually started quite well. Sandro Mazzola, who was a director when I was at the club, had a good chance, but Ronnie Simpson made an important diving save. We were all outraged when the referee awarded Inter a penalty-kick in the seventh minute. Jim Craig's challenge on Renato Cappellini seemed good, but, looking at it again, you could see it was very much a penalty-kick.

"Mazzola was Inter's star player around that time and he accepted the responsibility of taking the penalty-kicks. Credit where credit is due; he took that one against Celtic very well and scored quite comfortably, sending the keeper the wrong way. What was very interesting, though, was the way Celtic's players kept interchanging as they continued to move forward. Jimmy Johnstone was everywhere and even came close with a header which was well saved by Sarti. Willie Wallace and Stevie Chalmers had the ability to drop deep and Bobby Lennox continually switched wings.

"Celtic got the neutral fans on their side with their flair. They played with such skill and commitment to going

NINETY MINUTES FROM HISTORY...Celtic skipper Billy McNeill shakes hands with Inter Milan captain Armando Picchi just before kick-off in the European Cup Final in Lisbon on May 25, 1967. Referee Kurt Tschenscher looks on.

THE BIG SHOT... Tommy Gemmell thunders in the equaliser against Inter Milan with Armando Picchi helpless to intervene.

forward. They seemed to be strong in all departments, especially in centre midfield where they had Bobby Murdoch and Bertie Auld, of course. These two guys really complemented each other. Bobby was up and down, from penalty box to penalty box; a real dynamo. He was a great passer of the ball with either foot. Bertie could put his foot on the ball when the pace needed to be slowed down. He had a great footballing brain.

"I was also amazed at how far forward the full-backs were against the Italians. They were popping up on the edge of the penalty box all the time. I remember Tommy Gemmell, in particular, having a helluva shot and Sarti making a tremendous save from his volley in the first-half. It was a real screamer, but the keeper got down to his left to push it away."

Brady, a player of exquisite footballing ability who spent two years at Inter Milan as a player and just over two years at Celtic as manager from 1991 to 1993, could hardly believe what was unfolding in front of his eyes as he watched the action. "I think goalkeeper Ronnie Simpson showed how vigilant he was inasmuch as Celtic were pushing up in the search for the

BHOYS ZONE IN the European Cup Final, Celtic had a remarkable forty-two goal attempts against Inter Milan with twenty-six on target. There were nineteen efforts inside the penalty area with twenty-three outside the box.

equaliser and were always open at the back and vulnerable to one long ball that could present danger.

"That's precisely what happened when a defender thumped one straight down the middle from just inside his own box. Ronnie raced out of his area and gave everyone heart failure when he backheeled the ball to John Clark with an Inter Milan player breathing down his neck. It was an unbelievable bit of skill and, I suppose in a way, epitomised the spirit of the Celtic side that day.

"There was to be no goal for Celtic in that first-half, of course, but I believe Jock Stein would have told his players to carry on doing what they were doing. 'You've got Inter Milan on the rack,' he would have said. I think he might have encouraged more shots from outside the box because it was becoming increasingly more difficult to get in behind the Inter Milan defence.

"Several times it looked as though Celtic would score only for Sarti to keep them out. He made some truly stupendous saves that day and none more so than his one-handed save after the ball had been deflected past him from a shot by Tommy Gemmell. Somehow he got back to stop

STEVIE'S WONDER...Chalmers scores the most historic – and important – goal in Celtic's history as he claims the European Cup winner.

BEACH BHOYS...Celtic often took their players away to the Ayrshire coast to prepare for big games. Jim Craig, Tommy Gemmell, Billy McNeill, Bertie Auld and Stevie Chalmers enjoy the bracing conditions of Troon.

COOL, BHOY...Jock Stein wears shades as he arrives at an airport on one of his many trips with Celtic. His tactics often put other teams in the shade!

"But the Celtic players simply never allowed them to get out. The patience in Celtic's play in that game was something to be admired. They never got panicky because they were a goal down. They never got carried away. The unrelenting spirit throughout the team, as I have said, was magnificent.

"They kept passing away, coming forward and probing, looking for openings. And, in fact, it was good possession football that led to the equaliser. Again both full-backs were well forward with Jim Craig laying the ball back for Tommy Gemmell and he just buried it past Sarti. There was no way the goalkeeper was going to keep that effort out of his net.

"It was interesting to see how many heads went down among the ranks of the Inter Milan players when they went forward to restart the game. They knew it was going to be very, very difficult to stem the tide with twenty-seven minutes still to go. I think they knew then that the game was up."

Brady continued: "There was a move shortly after the equaliser when Tommy Gemmell got down the left again and his ball inside eventually broke in front of Bobby Murdoch about 25 yards from goal. He demonstrated the awesome shooting power he possessed in both feet when he hit it first-time with his so-called weaker left foot and Sarti was forced to make another miraculous save.

"Later in the second-half, we saw a cross from far out on the left by Tommy Gemmell. I hope I am not doing Tommy an injustice by saying it was a cross – he might say he was trying for goal – and Sarti made one of his few mistakes when he lost the flight of the ball. He misjudged it completely, but it hit the bar when it could so easily have dropped behind him.

"One of the most impressive things for me in that performance was the technique each and every player had. They were of a very high quality. I can remember watching a lot of football back then – it was like a drug to me as I was growing up. I watched a lot of Manchester United and Tottenham Hotspur on the television.

"I used to marvel at players such as George Best, Bobby Charlton, Denis Law, Pat Crerand, Jimmy Greaves, Pat Jennings and so on. The BBC used to show a lot of English football, but then along came this Celtic team and suddenly we were all Celtic fans!

the ball right on the line. Celtic claimed a goal, but it was a truly superb save.

"The second-half was more or less played in Inter's half which was quite amazing when you consider their reputation for counter-attacking. Obviously, it was something they were very good at because they played that way week in, week out. They got plenty of practice. Mazzola and Domenghini were especially dangerous going forward.

CELTIC forced ten corner-kicks against Inter Milan who didn't have a single one. Jock Stein's side were caught offside seven times as against the Italians' two. Both sides committed twenty fouls each.

"Few teams had the technique that Celtic possessed right throughout the side. This was undoubtedly a conscious decision by Jock Stein to get each and every one of his players to perform at a certain level. I still believe Celtic should have been ahead even before Stevie Chalmers scored the winner.

"They were denied a legitimate penalty-kick, as far as I am concerned. I remember it vividly. Tommy Gemmell got the ball across and Sarti and his defender got in a terrible mix-up and the ball broke to Willie Wallace. He was just about to knock it into the empty net when the goalkeeper wrapped his arms around one of his legs and quite deliberately pulled him down. No-one could believe the referee didn't immediately point to the spot.

"Well, the second goal just had to come, hadn't it? Without going overboard, it would have been a tragedy if Celtic hadn't won. I have never seen a team dominate a match so much. It could have been 5-1 or 6-1 at the end and no-one could have complained. However, with about five or so minutes to go, it was Tommy Gemmell once more getting down the left and again showing his wonderful ability at taking on players.

"He pushed the ball inside for Bobby Murdoch and he let fly. Stevie Chalmers was right in line with the effort and he guided it in with his instep from close range. The Italians actually appealed for offside, as you might expect, but film showed Stevie was well on.

"Justice was done. It was a victory for the good guys. It was a victory for football. Everything that Inter Milan stood for was wrong. It was wrong for them to deny their exceptionally skilful players such as Mazzola, Suarez and Jair the opportunity to express themselves in games. However, when they got a goal ahead, they fell back into deep defence and put up the shutters. It was all so negative.

"Helenio Herrera v. Jock Stein was an intriguing contest on a coaching level. Thankfully, Jock's philosophy won the day. Celtic really stopped the domination of European football by these stifling, frustrating, unattractive and unimaginative tactics.

"They did Europe a real favour in Lisbon. They put the smile back on the face of football."

Simpson; Craig, Gemmell; Murdoch, McNeill, Clark. Johnstone, Wallace, Chalmers, Auld and Lennox. ■

An extract from Alex Gordon's book 'The Lisbon Lions: The 40th Anniversary' which was published in 2007.

European Cup

September 28, 1966:
First Round: 1st leg:
CELTIC 2 Gemmell, McBride
ZURICH 0
Simpson; Gemmell, O'Neill; Murdoch, McNeill, Clark; Johnstone, McBride, Chalmers, Auld, Hughes.

October 5:
First Round: 2nd leg:
ZURICH 0
CELTIC 3 (Agg: 5-0) Gemmell (2, 1 pen), Chalmers
Simpson; Gemmell, O'Neill; Murdoch, McNeill, Clark; Johnstone, Lennox, Chalmers, Auld, Hughes.

November 30:
Second Round: 1st leg:
NANTES 1 Magny
CELTIC 3 McBride, Lennox, Chalmers
Simpson; Gemmell, O'Neill; Murdoch, McNeill, Clark; Johnstone, Chalmers, McBride, Lennox, Auld.

December 7:
Second Round: 2nd leg:
CELTIC 3 Johnstone, Chalmers, Lennox
NANTES 1 (Agg: 6-2) Georgin
Simpson; Gemmell, O'Neill; Murdoch, McNeill, Clark; Johnstone, Gallagher, Chalmers, Auld, Lennox.

March 1, 1967:
Quarter-final: 1st leg:
VOJVODINA NOVI SAD 1 Stanic
CELTIC 0
Simpson; Craig, Gemmell; Murdoch, McNeill, Clark; Johnstone, Lennox, Chalmers, Auld, Hughes.

March 8:
Quarter-final: 2nd leg:
CELTIC 2 Chalmers, McNeill
VOJVODINA 0 (Agg: 2-1)
Simpson; Craig, Gemmell; Murdoch, McNeill, Clark; Johnstone, Lennox, Chalmers, Gallagher, Hughes.

April 12:
Semi-final: 1st leg:
CELTIC 3 Johnstone, Wallace (2)
DUKLA PRAGUE 1 Strunc
Simpson; Craig, Gemmell; Murdoch, McNeill, Clark; Johnstone, Wallace, Chalmers, Auld, Hughes.

April 25:
Semi-final: 2nd leg:
DUKLA PRAGUE 0
CELTIC 0 (Agg: 3-1)
Simpson; Craig, Gemmell; Murdoch, McNeill, Clark; Johnstone, Wallace, Chalmers, Auld, Lennox.

May 25:
Final:
CELTIC 2 Gemmell, Chalmers
INTER MILAN 1 Mazzola (pen)
Simpson; Craig, Gemmell; Murdoch, McNeill, Clark; Johnstone, Wallace, Chalmers, Auld, Lennox.

Jock Stein
profile update

The secret of being a good manager is to keep the six players who hate you away from the five who are undecided.

JOCK STEIN was a man on a mission as he prepared his Celtic team for season 1968/69. Two trophies – the European Cup and the Scottish Cup – had been removed from the Parkhead trophy cabinet during the previous campaign.

And it was well known in the world of football Jock Stein was a bad loser; a very bad loser. To relinquish their grip on Europe's elite competition at the first hurdle hurt the pride of the manager. To have it virtually prised from his grasp following a bizarre encounter in the east end of Glasgow by a merely-competent Kiev Dynamo side was unacceptable.

Celtic lost the first leg 2-1 on home soil and, in controversial circumstances, drew 1-1 in Russia where they had 'goals' from Billy McNeill and John Hughes ruled out in mysterious conditions and, just to add insult to injury, they had Bobby Murdoch ordered off for the heinous crime of bouncing the ball after disagreeing with one of Italian referee Antonio Sbardella's many unfathomable decisions.

Their defence of the Scottish Cup in the 1967/68 season didn't get beyond the initial stage either. In January 1968 they succumbed 2-0 to Dunfermline at their own citadel in a Cup-tie marred by more contentious decisions by the match official, on this occasion Bobby Davidson, who would certainly never get a place on Stein's Christmas card list. The Airdrie whistler had the uncanny knack of upsetting the Celtic gaffer and the team's followers.

It appeared the holders had nullified a Hugh Robertson goal for the visitors. Jim Brogan caught the ball sweetly from about twenty-five yards and his first-time drive left his former team-mate, Danish keeper Bent Martin, motionless as it thumped into the net. Celtic Park erupted and not one Fife player complained, but, bewilderingly, it was disallowed.

Apparently, Bobby Lennox had been in an offside position. That was correct, but it was also accurate to point out that the player was in no way interfering with play. Celtic's protests fell on deaf ears.

It was all over when a wayward pass from young Davie Cattenach in the second-half was seized upon by the Fife team's striker Pat Gardner and Ronnie Simpson's late rush from goal couldn't avert disaster.

That bleak January afternoon saw the Dunfermline players celebrate like they had won the tournament and, in fact, they managed that feat late in April when they beat Hearts 3-1 in the final at Hampden on an extraordinary day, not only for them, but also Celtic.

With two league games to go as the season headed for a dramatic climax, Celtic were on top of the First Division table, albeit on goal average, as it was then before goal difference was introduced.

Celtic had scored 102 goals and conceded twenty-two as opposed to Rangers' eighty-nine for and thirty against. Stein's men had claimed thirteen more and conceded eight fewer. Their goal average was 4.64 compared with Rangers' 2.97. Celtic knew they could afford to win their remaining two games by the slenderest of margins and the

League Table Top Ten

P	Team	Pld	W	D	L	GF	GA	GD	Pts
1	**Celtic**	**34**	**23**	**8**	**3**	**89**	**32**	**57**	**54**
2	Rangers	34	21	7	6	81	32	49	49
3	Dunfermline Athletic	34	19	7	8	63	45	18	45
4	Kilmarnock	34	15	14	5	50	32	18	44
5	Dundee United	34	17	9	8	61	49	12	43
6	St Johnstone	34	16	5	13	66	59	7	37
7	Airdrieonians	34	13	11	10	46	44	2	37
8	Heart of Midlothian	34	14	8	12	52	54	−2	36
9	Dundee	34	10	12	12	47	48	−1	32
10	Morton	34	12	8	14	58	68	−10	32

League Cup Final

April 5, 1969: **CELTIC 6**   Wallace, Auld, Lennox (3), Craig
HIBS 2   O'Rourke, Stevenson

Fallon; Craig, Gemmell (sub: Clark); Murdoch, McNeill, Brogan; Johnstone, Wallace, Chalmers, Auld, Lennox.

Scottish Cup Final

April 26, 1969: **CELTIC 4**   McNeill, Lennox, Connelly, Chalmers
RANGERS 0

Fallon; Craig, Gemmell; Murdoch, McNeill, Brogan; Connelly, Wallace, Chalmers, Auld, Lennox.

BHOYS

AN end of an era was witnessed at Celtic Park on May 1, 1971 when the Lions appeared together for the last time. Ronnie Simpson, who had already announced his retirement, was in the line-up as it was led out by Billy McNeill, but he was replaced before the start by Evan Williams. Celtic beat Clyde 6-1 with three goals from Bobby Lennox, two from Willie Wallace and one from Stevie Chalmers.

ZONE

CHEERS...Jock Stein acknowledges the applause from the Celtic fans, something the manager got used to over the years.

THREE AMIGOS...Jock Stein has a chat with his good friend and Liverpool's legendary manager Bill Shankly as his captain Billy McNeill listens in. It was Shankly who burst into the dressing room in Lisbon after Celtic had won the European Cup in 1967 and declared excitedly: "John, you're immortal!"

championship would be theirs for the third successive season. Rangers could win two and match them on points, but only a miracle would pull things around in their favour as far as goal average was concerned.

That season's championship had ebbed and flowed in a truly memorable campaign. With one game to go, Rangers were due to play Aberdeen at Ibrox on Cup Final day – April 27 – and faced the genuine prospect of going through the entire league programme, all thirty-four games, without defeat and still not winning the title. That would have been one for the history books.

Stein was at Hampden that afternoon to watch his old club Dunfermline, the team who had abruptly cut short Celtic's interest in the tournament, face Hearts. Two goals from Pat Gardner and a penalty-kick from Ian Lister gave the Fifers a 3-1 triumph. It seemed a lifetime ago that Stein had been congratulating his Dunfermline players after their replay success in the competition over Celtic; in fact, it had been seven years minus a day.

The Celtic manager stood to applaud when a national newspaper reporter gave him the news. "Rangers have lost 3-2 at Ibrox." Stein asked: "Are you certain?" He was assured the Pittodrie side had scored a last-minute winner. Rangers had definitely gone down 3-2.

Ignoring the limp that had ended his playing career, Stein attempted to bound down the Hampden steps and his ankle almost buckled under his weight. He stumbled, got his bearings and raced off to spread the news. "This has been a great day," he said. Who could argue?

Celtic realised they could now afford to lose their last league game against Dunfermline the following midweek and still keep their crown. It was a joint celebration in Fife; the champions v. the Cup winners and it was the hottest ticket in town. The game attracted East End Park's official

record attendance of 27,816, but it was estimated some 5,000 fans also crammed into the packed surroundings.

Bobby Lennox had scored in every one of Celtic's last eleven games, amassing an extraordinary eighteen goals, as he prepared for the duel in Dunfermline. He had also scored in the opening 3-0 win over Clyde in September. Now he was about to finish what he had started.

In typical style, he did just that. Lennox flashed in two goals in a 2-1 victory to bring home a third successive title, the first time the feat had been achieved since 1935. By comparison, the treble the following season seemed a bit more sedate.

In 1967/68, Celtic won the championship with sixty-three points, a record post-war total. Twelve months later, they took the title with nine points fewer. Tommy Gemmell walloped in the equaliser in a 2-2 stalemate against Kilmarnock at Rugby Park on April 21, 1969 for the goal that brought in title No.4.

The two back-to-back League Cup Finals brought a sixteen-goal avalanche, with a 5-3 victory over Dundee followed by a 6-2 triumph over Hibs. And the disappointment against Dunfermline was forgotten when Celtic ran amok in the Scottish Cup Final, pulverising their way to a 4-0 victory over their Ibrox rivals.

Stein was reasonably satisfied with his second treble in three years and he was often asked how he continued to instill such enthusiasm, hunger and drive in his team, season after season. He contemplated for a moment before delivering the classic response.

"The secret of being a good manager is to keep the six players who hate you away from the five who are undecided."

Jock Stein did possess a sense of humour, but no-one knew for certain if he was joking or serious on this particular occasion. ■

FRIENDS REUNITED...Jock Stein and Sir Alex Ferguson share a joke on the training field during their days with the Scotland international squad. Stein brought in the iconic Manchester United boss as his assistant in the eighties. Ferguson always insisted: "Jock Stein was the finest football manager in Britain."

BHOYS

BERTIE AULD left Celtic on a free transfer for Hibs on May 6, 1971. Shortly afterwards Stevie Chalmers and John Clark left for Morton and, within a year, Tommy Gemmell had joined Nottingham Forest, Willie Wallace and John Hughes moved to Crystal Palace and Jim Craig signed for South African side Hellenic.

ZONE

Six of the Best

CELTIC 2
DUNDEE UNITED 0
(October 5, 1968)

THE Tannadice outfit arrived at Parkhead attempting to preserve their unbeaten record, but a duo of net-bursting strikes from Bobby Murdoch, three minutes after the interval, and Tommy Gemmell, nine minutes from time, sent them home pointless.

An amazing flashpoint concerning temperamental winger Jimmy Johnstone and manager Jock Stein thirteen minutes from the end dominated the headlines afterwards. The situation blew up when the Celtic boss decided to replace an out-of-sorts Johnstone with substitute George Connelly. Clearly, Jinky wasn't quite in sync with Big Jock's pattern of thought.

As one newspaper reporter put it: "It was with some reluctance that Johnstone left the field after, at first, appearing to disregard the instructions from his manager. He appeared to pass some comment towards the dug-out while tearing at his shirt. Mr Stein quickly followed the player into the pavilion."

The 46,000 supporters in attendance that day must have been wondering what on earth was going on between the team's star player and the manager outwith their vision. Johnstone put it this way: "As soon as I did it, I thought: 'My God! What have I done?' I belted up the tunnel as fast as I could, but I knew he would be right behind me. My first notion was to run straight through the front door without changing and just disappear forever. I got into the dressing room and locked the door behind me.

"I heard him kicking the door then battering it with his fist. I shouted out: 'I'll let you in if you promise not to hit me!' Then the battering suddenly stopped and there was a kind of silence and – would you believe it? – he burst out laughing at what I had said. He just laughed and I heard him walking away because, of course, the game was still going on."

Immediately after the match action, the fans' favourite was told forcibly by the directors that Celtic would not tolerate such misbehaviour from one of their players and Johnstone was promptly suspended for seven days. The wee winger told friends he readily accepted the punishment because it was a lot better than "being thumped by Big Jock".

Simpson; Craig, Gemmell; Murdoch, McNeill, Brogan; Johnstone (sub: Connelly), Wallace, Chalmers, McBride and Hughes.

HOOP, HOOP, HOORAY... the incomparable Jimmy Johnstone, voted Celtic's Greatest-Ever Player by the fans, and dependable right-back Jim Craig race out of the Parkhead tunnel as they prepare for another entertaining encounter. Things were never dull when Wee Jinky was around!

HIBS 2
CELTIC 5
(November 30, 1968)

CELTIC staged the most breathtaking revival of the season to hammer Hibs into submission in an annual fixture that appeared to be reserved for the dramatic and the extraordinary.

Only eleven minutes remained with the Easter Road side winning 2-1 and looking poised for a hard-fought victory. They had staged their own comeback following Tommy Gemmell's pummelled penalty-kick in the eighth minute that almost ripped the net from its stanchion behind keeper Willie Wilson.

Incredibly, it was old Celtic favourite Joe McBride who piled on the pressure. The strongman centre-forward had been allowed to leave Parkhead by Jock Stein, an unusually hasty decision by the manager, and there was little doubt the player had a point to prove. He struck in the 23rd minute and the enthralling spectacle was deadlocked for the next 51 minutes until the Edinburgh outfit were awarded a penalty-kick. Left-back Joe Davis was Hibs' version of Tommy Gemmell and he took all their spot-kicks. He rarely missed and he didn't disappoint the home support as he calmly sidefooted his effort wide of John Fallon, deputising for the injured Ronnie Simpson.

With the clock ticking down, Billy McNeill, as ever playing a captain's part, launched a header behind the stranded Wilson in the 79th minute. The fightback was on in earnest and Hibs were contemptuously brushed aside as the champions sensed blood. Merely sixty seconds after McNeill's leveller, John Hughes, who had been in rampaging form throughout the afternoon, clubbed in the third.

The home players were still reeling when, two minutes later, Bobby Lennox nipped in for a fourth goal. Celtic still weren't satisfied, though, and the relentless Hughes, affectionately known to the fans as Yogi Bear, after the character in the TV cartoon of the era, barged his way through the retreating rearguard before banging No.5 behind the bewildered Wilson.

The triumph was crucial as it moved Celtic onto 22 points from thirteen games – remember, these were the days of two points for a win – two ahead of Dundee United. Rangers were struggling in sixth place, six points adrift of the Parkhead pacesetters.

Fallon; Craig, Gemmell; Murdoch, McNeill, Brogan; Johnstone, Callaghan, Wallace (sub: Chalmers), Lennox and Hughes. ▶

BHOYS ZONE

CELTIC won twenty-three of their thirty-four First Division games in season 1968/69 to lift their fourth successive championship.

YOGI BEAR...Celtic's powerful attacker John Hughes was named after the popular TV American cartoon character of the sixties. However, the opposition never found it a laughing matter when the hooped juggernaut got into his stride. He scored 189 goals in his prolific Celtic career.

CELTIC 3
DUNFERMLINE 1
(January 4, 1969)

CELTIC went into this confrontation nursing a sense of injustice following the game against Rangers at Ibrox only two days earlier. Jock Stein and his players were incensed when the referee awarded a penalty-kick to Rangers on the hour mark. The match official adjudged Billy McNeill had deliberately used his hand to stop a shot from Willie Henderson.

Despite the long and loud protestations from the skipper and his team-mates, referee Archie Webster wasn't impressed. He waved them away and, once the furore had ebbed, John Greig stepped up to take the kick. The home skipper was not well-known for his finesse and he simply bludgeoned the ball high and straight as John Fallon elected to pick a corner.

Stein had his players primed to respond against the Fifers and they didn't let him down in front of 43,508 spectators. Willie Wallace, who had struggled to make an impression at Ibrox, settled the nerves with the opening goal inside sixty seconds, neatly converting past the exposed Willie Duff, in the Dunfermline goal. And it was Wallace who doubled his team's advantage in the ninth minute with another typical chance-snatcher's opportunity.

However, the East End Park line-up proved to be tricky customers and had emphasised their menace the previous year when they knocked holders Celtic out of the Scottish Cup with a 2-0 success in Glasgow on their way to winning the silverware. They could make life uncomfortable and so it proved in the twentieth minute when impish right-winger Alex Edwards, a box of tricks in the Jimmy Johnstone mould, pulled one back.

There was never any love lost between Jock Stein and his opposite number George Farm and there was the usual tension when their teams locked horns. The second-half was fiercely contested until Bobby Lennox, a prince among penalty-box predators, materialised in space and tucked the third and decisive goal behind Duff.

Celtic then introduced Jimmy Johnstone as a substitute for Lennox and the winger went straight to his usual berth on the right with John Hughes switching to the left. The tactical manoeuvre befuddled Farm and the points were in the bag.

Fallon; Craig, Gemmell; Murdoch, McNeill, Brogan; Hughes, Wallace, Chalmers, Callaghan and Lennox (sub: Johnstone).

IN GEAR...Jimmy Johnstone was known for his trickery, but he was also a dedicated trainer.

THE DEFENCE DOESN'T REST...Celtic were hailed as an attacking team, but they could defend, too, as Tommy Gemmell and Jim Brogan prove here against Falkirk with keeper Ronnie Simpson grounded.

ABERDEEN 1
CELTIC 3
(January 11, 1969)

CELTIC travelled to Pittodrie in defiant mood to meet a worthy adversary. Sparks often flew when these teams shared a football pitch and this confrontation promised to be no different. However, on this occasion, the visitors won with surprising ease at the home of long-term rivals.

Juggernaut John Hughes enjoyed the Dons' huge playing surface as he roamed the left wing, probing patiently for openings before exploding into action, his powerful frame carrying all before him. The 6ft 2in forward was remarkably nimble for such a tall and muscular character. Amazingly, though, he was gifted with mesmerising close control and, when he got into his stride, he was virtually unstoppable.

Opponents realised they were in for a torrid ninety minutes when Big Yogi was at the peak of his powers. He was a one-man demolition squad when he was in the mood.

Unfortunately, for the Dons, on a cold, blustery afternoon in the north, Celtic's personality forward raced on to the frozen-solid playing surface with the sole intention of teasing, tormenting and, inevitably, terrorising their defence. He opened the scoring in the third minute and the pattern for the following eighty-seven minutes had been set.

Willie Wallace had regained his form, too, and the man known as Wispy was also proving to be a thorn in the Aberdeen rearguard. On this occasion, the former Hearts player was deployed smack in the middle of the attack alongside Bobby Lennox. Jimmy Johnstone occupied the outside-right berth and left-sided Tommy Callaghan, who had arrived in a £35,000 transfer from Dunfermline, linked up with Bobby Murdoch in the middle of the park.

It was Wallace who netted the second goal just before the half-hour mark and Eddie Turnbull's team were unable to fashion a way back into the game. And Wallace made a telling contribution to the goal that brought the opponents to their knees. He glanced in a header and panicking defender Henning Boel deflected the ball past his own keeper, Ernie McGarr, in the sixty-second minute. Jim Forrest snatched a late consolation effort, but the points were already heading for the east end of Glasgow.

Simpson; Craig, Gemmell; Murdoch, McNeill, Brogan; Johnstone, Wallace, Callaghan, Lennox and Hughes.

CELTIC 5
HEARTS 0
(February 1, 1969)

RONNIE SIMPSON was the man Celtic had to thank for their one-goal interval lead against a Tynecastle side primed for counter-attack. It had all been going according to the script when Bobby Lennox fired the opening goal behind Jim Cruickshank in the thirteenth minute.

However, the visitors from Edinburgh were not about to wave the white flag of surrender as they hit on the break with verve and vigour. Goalkeeper Simpson, so often a spectator as his team-mates laid siege to their opponents' goal, was called into action to make three smart saves with Hearts somehow finding gaps between Billy McNeill and Jim Brogan in Celtic's normally reliable and robust central defence.

Whatever Jock Stein had to say to his troops over their half-time cuppa it worked! Jim Craig remembered an incident during an interval when the far-from-impressed manager laid into his players to let them know the extent of his dissatisfaction about their performance in the first forty-five minutes of one particular outing.

Craig wasn't playing that day, but was in the dressing room as Stein had his say. The European Cup-winning right-back said: "Big Jock was going round everyone and telling them where they were going wrong. After sweeping through the entire team he turned to me and said: 'I don't know why you're so smug. You're not even good enough to get into this side.' What could I say?"

BHOYS ZONE

VETERAN keeper Ronnie Simpson's persistent shoulder injury restricted the fans' favourite to twenty-three outings in all competitions. Simpson, at the age of thirty-nine, retired the following season – his last game was a 2-1 League Cup semi-final replay victory over Ayr United on October 13, 1969.

Celtic took the field in slightly more aggressive fashion for the second period and suddenly Cruickshank was the busiest man on the park as he attempted to repel wave after wave of attack. Willie Wallace hit a second goal ten minutes after the turnaround and Bobby Murdoch zipped in a third eight minutes later.

Jimmy Johnstone pirouetted onto the scene to roll in a fourth goal and the champions were so much in command that defensive anchorman Brogan, who had taken over the sweeper's role from John Clark, joined in the attack to belt No.5 past the overworked and exhausted Cruickshank. Simpson, on the other hand, could have taken out a deckchair and settled down with a good book for the second-half as he was so rarely called into action. When Big Jock talked, players listened!

Simpson; Craig, Gemmell; Murdoch, McNeill, Brogan; Johnstone, Lennox, Wallace, Chalmers and Auld.

NET PROFIT...Jimmy Johnstone could make and take goals as he demonstrates with a close-range effort against Morton keeper Andy Crawford with defender Hugh Strachan vainly appealing for offside.

FLASH HARRY...Jock Stein brought in Harry Hood from Clyde during the season and he was a shrewd acquisition. Here he nets against Morton keeper Erik Sorensen with defenders John Lavelle and Davie Hayes helpless.

KILMARNOCK 2
CELTIC 2
(April 21, 1969)

CAVALIER defender Tommy Gemmell, a genuine world-class performer, will be forever remembered and revered for his almighty whack that sent the ball hurtling into the roof of Giuliano Sarti's net for Celtic's equaliser against Inter Milan on their way to the magnificent 2-1 European Cup triumph in Lisbon on May 25, 1967.

Gemmell enjoyed the sensation of scoring in the grand finale of Europe's elite tournament so much he staged an action replay three years later when he flashed a wicked twenty-five yard howitzer into the Feyenoord rigging in the San Siro Stadium in Milan. Alas, on this occasion, there was no happy ending as the Dutch won 2-1 with a goal three minutes from the end of extra-time.

How many remember, though, a typical long-range goal from the extravagantly-gifted left-back that won Celtic their fourth successive title? Glorious Gemmell hit the headlines once more in a midweek game against Kilmarnock at Rugby Park when Jock Stein's team once again demonstrated their stubborn refusal to admit defeat even when the alarm bells were ringing loud and clear. The Parkhead men arrived in Ayrshire knowing a solitary point would be enough to claim the crown.

However, after only half-an-hour, that eventuality might have looked beyond them as they trailed 2-0 to a dangerous Killie outfit. In the eighth minute, John Fallon was retrieving the ball from the back of the net after Eddie Morrison flicked home a Tommy McLean cross. In the thirtieth minute, the Celtic keeper was required to repeat the function. This time Gerry Queen was the scorer and the home side held onto their advantage until the interval.

Obviously, it was time for boss Stein to go to work on his players. Big Jock had the ability to cajole and coax a performance out of an individual. Other times, he reckoned fierce criticism might be the key to activate a character. Once again, a rejuvenated set of players took the pitch for the second instalment in another tale in Celtic folklore. Killie were resolute as they repelled the raids of their rivals, the attacks growing more frantic as the half wore on.

Suddenly, there was hope from an unexpected source. Bobby Murdoch flighted in a high ball and it was diverted into his own net by the Ayrshire team's skipper Frank Beattie. Game on!

With only a handful of seconds remaining, the ball was worked across to the menacing Gemmell about ten yards outside the penalty area. Distance was never a barrier for the club's idolised extrovert. His timing, as ever, was impeccable as he smacked the ball first-time with his right foot and it was a blur as it fizzed low past the static Sandy McLaughlin.

Job done! And Championship Number Four in the history books!

Fallon; Craig, Gemmell; Murdoch, McNeill, Clark; Johnstone, Callaghan (sub: Lennox), Wallace, Chalmers and Hood. ▪

League Results

September 7, 1968:
CLYDE 0
CELTIC 3   Brogan, Lennox, Gemmell (pen)
Simpson; Craig, Gemmell; Brogan, McNeill, Clark; Johnstone (sub: Chalmers), Lennox, McBride, Connelly, Hughes.

September 14:   **CELTIC 2**   Wallace (2)
RANGERS 4   Persson, Johnston (2), Penman
Simpson; Gemmell, O'Neill; Brogan, McNeill, Clark; Johnstone, Lennox, Wallace, Connelly (sub: Chalmers), Hughes.

September 21:   **DUNFERMLINE 1**   Fraser
CELTIC 1   Johnstone
Simpson; Craig, Gemmell; Murdoch, McNeill, Brogan; Johnstone, Wallace, Chalmers, Lennox, Hughes.

September 28:   **CELTIC 2**   Connelly, Lennox
ABERDEEN 1   Rae
Simpson; Craig, Gemmell; Murdoch, McNeill, Brogan; Johnstone, Lennox, Wallace, Connelly, Hughes.

October 5:   **CELTIC 2**   Murdoch, Gemmell
DUNDEE UNITED 0
Simpson; Craig, Gemmell; Murdoch, McNeill, Brogan; Johnstone (sub: Connelly), Wallace, Chalmers, McBride, Hughes.

October 12:   **HEARTS 0**
CELTIC 1   Chalmers
Simpson; Craig, Gemmell; Clark, McNeill, Brogan; Connelly, Wallace, McBride, Chalmers, Lennox.

October 19:   **CELTIC 2**   Lennox, McNeill
ST JOHNSTONE 1   Coburn
Simpson; Craig, Gemmell; Clark, McNeill, Brogan; Johnstone, Connelly, Chalmers, Lennox, Hughes.

October 26:   **MORTON 1**   Harper
CELTIC 1   McBride
Simpson; Craig, Gemmell; Murdoch, McNeill, Brogan; Johnstone, McBride, Wallace, Lennox, Hughes.

November 2:   **CELTIC 3**   Johnstone , Chalmers (2)
DUNDEE 1   Campbell
Simpson; Craig, Gemmell; Murdoch, McNeill, Brogan; Johnstone, Wallace, Chalmers, Lennox, Hughes.

November 9:   **ARBROATH 0**
CELTIC 5   Chalmers (3), McNeill, Wallace
Fallon; Craig, Gemmell; Murdoch, McNeill, Brogan; Johnstone, Wallace, Chalmers, Lennox (sub: Auld), Hughes.

November 23:   **PARTICK THISTLE 0**
CELTIC 4   Hughes (2), Callaghan, Lennox
Fallon; Craig, Gemmell; Murdoch, McNeill, Brogan; Johnstone, Lennox, Chalmers (sub: Wallace), Callaghan, Hughes.

November 30:   **HIBS 2**   McBride, Davis (pen)
CELTIC 5   Gemmell (pen), McNeill, Hughes (2), Lennox
Fallon; Craig, Gemmell; Murdoch, McNeill, Brogan; Johnstone, Callaghan, Wallace (sub: Chalmers), Lennox, Hughes.

December 7:   **CELTIC 5**   Chalmers (2), Johnstone, Hughes, Gemmell (pen)
ST MIRREN 0
Fallon; Craig, Gemmell; Murdoch, McNeill, Brogan; Johnstone, Lennox, Chalmers, Callaghan, Hughes (sub: Wallace).

December 14:   **FALKIRK 0**
CELTIC 0
Fallon; Craig, Gemmell; Murdoch, McNeill, Brogan; Johnstone, Lennox, Wallace, Callaghan, Hughes.

December 21:   **CELTIC 1**   Chalmers
KILMARNOCK 1   McIlroy
Fallon; Craig, Gemmell; Murdoch, McNeill, Brogan; Johnstone, Callaghan, Chalmers, Auld, Hughes.

December 28:   **AIRDRIE 0**
CELTIC 0
Fallon; Craig, Gemmell; Murdoch, McNeill, Brogan; Johnstone, Wallace, Hughes, Chalmers, Lennox.

January 1, 1969:   **CELTIC 5**   Callaghan (2), Gemmell (pen), Wallace, Lennox
CLYDE 0
Fallon; Craig, Gemmell; Murdoch, McNeill, Brogan (sub: Auld); Johnstone, Lennox, Wallace, Callaghan, Hughes.

January 2:   **RANGERS 1**   Greig (pen)
CELTIC 0
Fallon; Craig, Gemmell; Brogan, McNeill, Clark; Johnstone, Murdoch, Wallace (sub: Chalmers), Lennox, Hughes.

January 4:   **CELTIC 3**   Wallace (2), Lennox
DUNFERMLINE 1   Edwards
Fallon; Craig, Gemmell; Murdoch, McNeill, Brogan; Hughes, Wallace, Chalmers, Callaghan, Lennox (sub: Johnstone).

January 11:   **ABERDEEN 1**   Forrest
CELTIC 3   Hughes, Wallace, Boel (og)
Simpson; Craig, Gemmell; Murdoch, McNeill, Brogan; Johnstone, Callaghan, Wallace, Lennox, Hughes.

January 18:   **DUNDEE UNITED 1**   Mitchell
CELTIC 3   Lennox, Hughes, McMahon
Simpson; Craig, Gemmell; Murdoch, McNeill, Brogan; Johnstone (sub: McMahon), Callaghan, Wallace, Lennox, Hughes.

February 1: **CELTIC 5** Lennox, Wallace, Murdoch, Johnstone, Brogan

HEARTS 0

Simpson; Craig, Gemmell; Murdoch, McNeill, Brogan; Johnstone, Lennox, Wallace, Chalmers, Auld.

March 5: **CELTIC 7** Wallace (3), Chalmers (2), Johnstone, Hughes

ARBROATH 1 Bruce

Fallon; Craig, Gemmell; Murdoch (sub: Auld), McNeill, Brogan; Johnstone, Wallace, Chalmers, Callaghan, Hughes.

March 8: **RAITH ROVERS 1** Wallace

CELTIC 3 Wallace (2), Auld

Fallon; Craig, Gemmell; Murdoch, McNeill, Brogan; Johnstone, Lennox, Wallace, Callaghan (sub: Auld), Hughes.

March 15: **CELTIC 1** Hughes

PARTICK THISTLE 0

Fallon; Craig, Gemmell; Murdoch, McNeill, Brogan; Johnstone, Chalmers, Wallace, Auld, Hughes.

March 24: **CELTIC 1** Wallace

HIBS 1 McBride

Fallon; Craig, O'Neill; Murdoch, McNeill, Brogan; Johnstone, Lennox, Wallace, Auld, Hughes.

March 29: **ST MIRREN 0**

CELTIC 3 Craig, Hughes, Hood

Fallon; Craig, Gemmell; Murdoch, McNeill, Brogan; Johnstone, Hood, Wallace, Lennox, Hughes (sub: Callaghan).

April 1: **ST JOHNSTONE 2** Hall, Connolly

CELTIC 3 Wallace, Gemmell, Hood

Fallon; Craig, Gemmell; Murdoch, McNeill, Brogan; Johnstone, Hood, Wallace, Lennox, Hughes (sub: Clark).

April 9: **CELTIC 5** Wallace (2, 1pen), Hood, Lennox (2)

FALKIRK 2 McLaughlin (2)

Fallon; Craig, O'Neill; Murdoch, McNeill, Clark; Johnstone, Wallace, Hood, Auld (sub: Callaghan), Lennox.

April 19: **CELTIC 2** Gemmell (pen), Lennox

AIRDRIE 2 McPheat, Marshall

Fallon; Craig, Gemmell; Murdoch, McNeill, Brogan; Johnstone, Hood, Wallace, Auld, Lennox.

April 21: **KILMARNOCK 2** Morrison, Queen

CELTIC 2 Beattie (og), Gemmell

Fallon; Craig, Gemmell; Murdoch, McNeill, Clark; Johnstone, Callaghan (sub: Lennox), Wallace, Chalmers, Hood.

April 28: **CELTIC 2** Wallace, Hood

MORTON 4 Bartram (3), Harper

Fallon; Cattenach, Gemmell; Murdoch, McNeill, Clark; Connelly (sub: Callaghan), Chalmers, Wallace, Hood, Auld.

May 1: **DUNDEE 1** Murdoch (og)

CELTIC 2 Macari, Hood

Fallon; Craig, O'Neill; Murdoch, McNeill, Clark; Chalmers, Wallace, Hood, Auld, Macari.

European Cup Results

September 18, 1968: First Round: 1st leg:

ST ETIENNE 2 Keita, Revelli

CELTIC 0

Simpson; Craig, Gemmell; Brogan, McNeill, Clark; Johnstone, Connelly, Wallace, Lennox, Hughes.

October 2: 2nd leg:

CELTIC 4 Gemmell (pen), Craig, Chalmers, McBride

ST ETIENNE 0 (Agg: 4-2)

Simpson; Craig, Gemmell; Murdoch, McNeill, Brogan; Johnstone, Wallace, Chalmers, McBride, Hughes.

November 13: Second Round: 1st leg:

CELTIC 5 Murdoch, Johnstone (2), Lennox, Wallace

RED STAR BELGRADE 1 Lazervic

Fallon; Craig, Gemmell; Murdoch, McNeill, Brogan; Johnstone, Wallace, Chalmers, Lennox, Hughes.

November 27: 2nd leg:

RED STAR BELGRADE 1 Ostojic

CELTIC 1 (Agg: 6-2) Wallace

Fallon; Craig, Gemmell; Brogan, McNeill, Clark; Connelly, Lennox, Chalmers (sub: Wallace), Murdoch, Hughes.

February 19, 1969: Quarter-final: 1st leg:

AC MILAN 0

CELTIC 0

Fallon; Craig, Gemmell; Clark, McNeill, Brogan (sub: Auld); Johnstone, Murdoch, Wallace, Lennox, Hughes.

March 12: 2nd leg:

CELTIC 0

AC MILAN 1 (Agg: 0-1) Prati

Fallon; Craig, Gemmell; Brogan (Auld), McNeill, Clark; Johnstone, Wallace, Chalmers, Murdoch, Hughes.

Two Trophies in One Day

CELTIC 6
HIBS 2
(April 5, 1969)

THIS was a day in history when smart observers claimed Celtic won TWO trophies on the same afternoon. A sizzling hat-trick from Bobby Lennox helped his team dismantle their Edinburgh opponents on a gloriously sunny afternoon at Hampden Park.

Elsewhere, though, a result emerged that virtually handed the Parkhead side their fourth successive First Division championship to sit nicely with their fourth League Cup on the bounce. Nearest challengers Rangers collapsed to a 2-1 upset against Dundee United at Tannadice and, while it's true the Ibrox side's loss went a long way to guaranteeing Celtic the crown yet again, the title was not finally settled until the 2-2 draw with Kilmarnock at Rugby Park on April 21.

Two league games later after the dust had settled on another exhilarating campaign, Jock Stein's side sat comfortably in pole position with fifty-four points from thirty-four games, five more than their Ibrox rivals.

The only thing on the Celtic manager's mind on April 5, though, was the League Cup confrontation against an Easter

Road side that had eked out a 1-1 draw in Glasgow the previous month. Hibs were the chameleons of Scottish football. One week, awesome; the next, awful. They would complete the league season in joint twelfth place alongside Clyde. Remarkably, considering their playing resources, they lost fifteen games.

And yet they could point to quality players among their ranks such as reliable goalkeeper Thomson Allan, who would go to the 1974 World Cup Finals as the Scotland back-up to David Harvey, Pat Stanton, who would enjoy an Indian Summer at Parkhead, John Blackley, an international defender, astute midfielder Peter Cormack, who would go onto play for Liverpool, and snake-hipped winger Peter Marinello, who, only nine months later, joined Arsenal for £100,000, a phenomenal amount for a Scottish player at the time.

For twenty-three minutes they kept an eager Celtic side at bay. Inside an hour, though, they had conceded six goals and were in football's equivalent of hell. Willie Wallace drew first blood when Bertie Auld, with his usual precision, curled a free-kick into the penalty area. Stanton managed to head clear, but the ball dropped straight at the feet of Wallace who rattled it through a ruck of players and beyond the reach of Allan.

Auld was enjoying the occasion as he strutted around the immaculate playing surface, spraying passes hither and yon as he probed for weaknesses in his opponents' defence. Not content with exploiting the gaps for his team-mates, the masterful Auld decided to add his name to the scoresheet. On the half-hour mark, he released Stevie Chalmers who scurried down the left before pitching over a teasing cross. Auld struck it first time with his left foot and the next time Allan saw the ball was when he was fishing it from the back of his net.

The Hibs players were looking forward to the sanctuary of their dressing room at half-time when lightning-swift Lennox struck for the third goal. Nothing could have been simpler. Jimmy Johnstone zipped in a right-wing corner-kick to the near-post and Lennox bolted in ahead of the massed ranks to get the merest of touches with his head to glide the ball away from an open-mouthed Allan. Was there any point in restarting the game for the second period? Hibs, as everyone in the 74,240 crowd would surely have atested, were a beaten team.

Thirteen minutes after the turnaround, Auld split the Edinburgh side's back lot and Lennox – "I'm convinced he

REST AND NO PLAY...for the time being! A rare image of Bobby Lennox taking it easy on the beach at Saltcoats.

League Cup

Group stages

August 10, 1968:   **RANGERS 0**
                   CELTIC 2   Wallace (2)
Simpson; Gemmell, O'Neill; Murdoch, McNeill, Brogan; Connelly (sub: Clark), Johnstone, Wallace, Lennox, Hughes.

August 14:   **CELTIC 4**   Wallace, Hughes, Murdoch, Gemmell (pen)
             MORTON 1   Mason
Simpson; Gemmell, O'Neill; Murdoch, McNeill, Brogan (sub: Macari); Johnstone, Connelly, Wallace, Lennox, Hughes.

August 17:   **CELTIC 4**   Wallace (4)
             PARTICK THISTLE 0
Simpson; Gemmell, O'Neill; Murdoch, McNeill, Brogan; Johnstone, Connelly (sub: Auld), Wallace, Lennox, Hughes.

August 24:   **CELTIC 1**   Wallace
             RANGERS 0
Simpson; Gemmell, O'Neill; Murdoch, McNeill, Brogan; Johnstone, Connelly, Wallace, Lennox, Hughes.

August 28:   **MORTON 0**
             CELTIC 3   Wallace, Lennox, Hughes
Fallon; Gemmell. O'Neill; Murdoch, McNeill, Brogan; Johnstone, Lennox, Wallace, Connelly, Hughes.

August 31:   **PARTICK THISTLE 1**   O'Neill,
             CELTIC 6   Lennox (5), Cumming (og)
Fallon; Craig, O'Neill; Murdoch, McNeill, Brogan; Johnstone, Lennox, Wallace, Connelly, Hughes.

September 11:   Quarter-finals: 1st leg:
                CELTIC 10   Chalmers (5), Lennox (5)
                HAMILTON ACCIES 0
Simpson; Craig, Gemmell; Brogan, McNeill, Clark; Macari, Lennox, McBride, Chalmers, Hughes (sub: Johnstone).

September 25:   2nd leg:
                HAMILTON ACCIES 2   Lawlor, Halpin
                CELTIC 4   McBride (2), McMahon, Clark
Wraith; Craig, Gorman; Connelly, Hay, Clark; McMahon, McBride, Quinn, Gallagher (sub: Dalglish), Macari.

October 9:   Semi-final:
             CELTIC 1   Connelly
             CLYDE 0
Simpson; Craig, Gemmell; Murdoch, McNeill, Brogan; Lennox, Wallace, Chalmers, McBride (sub: Connelly), Hughes.

April 5, 1969:   Cup Final:
                 CELTIC 6   Wallace, Auld, Lennox (3), Craig
                 HIBS 2   O'Rourke, Stevenson
Fallon; Craig, Gemmell (sub: Clark); Murdoch, McNeill, Brogan; Johnstone, Wallace, Chalmers, Auld, Lennox.

was born fast," Danny McGrain was fond of saying – waltzed onto the pass, leaving gasping defenders in his slipstream, and drew Allan from his line before stroking the ball into the vacant net. If it had been a boxing match, the referee would have put the Edinburgh players out of their misery. No such luck in this particular sport, however. Celtic continued the trek towards Allan, who must have wondered about the wisdom of becoming a netminder.

Lennox completed his trio in the seventy-third minute and Jim Craig, who scored goals with the regularity of a sighting of Hally's Comet, slotted in the sixth goal from a tight angle. Jock Stein decided to give John Clark some exercise and sent him on for Tommy Gemmell. The defender's arrival coincided with two late goals from Hibs, Jimmy O'Rourke netting in the eighty-second minute and Eric Stevenson five minutes later. Apparently, Clark didn't even blush as he picked up his winner's medal.

The game had been due to take place in October, but had to be delayed because of a fire in the Hampden stand. Three weeks later, Celtic would return to the national stadium to take on Rangers in the Scottish Cup Final.

Who would have bet on another four-goal winning margin for Jock Stein's team? A special and extraordinary season in the club's history.

Fallon; Craig, Gemmell (sub: Clark); Murdoch, McNeill, Brogan; Johnstone, Wallace, Chalmers, Auld and Lennox. ∎

Connelly is Treble Ace

CELTIC 4
RANGERS 0
(April 26, 1969)

GEORGE CONNELLY **had just turned twenty years of age the previous month and was a relatively unknown quantity among the Celtic first team squad.**

However, after his supreme appearance in the Scottish Cup Final against Rangers at Hampden in 1969, the Fifer was the player most acclaimed by the delighted followers of the newly-crowned treble winners. Connelly, though, should have been nowhere near the Parkhead first team that eventful afternoon when Jock Stein's all-conquering line-up completed their second silverware clean sweep in three years.

A suspension to Jimmy Johnstone opened the door for the precocious youngster as the Celtic manager revamped his tactics against his club's obstinate foes from Govan. In fact, Rangers had struck a rich vein of form nearing the end of the season and had decimated a strong Aberdeen line-up 6-1 in the Scottish Cup semi-final at Parkhead on the same afternoon Stein's men had overcome Morton 4-1 at the national stadium.

The bookies, those characters with cigars the same size as rolled umbrellas and professionals who rarely indulged in errors where money is concerned, actually made the Ibrox outfit favourites to lift the trophy. Certainly, history was on Rangers' side – they had yet to be defeated in a Scottish Cup Final for forty years. Their Parkhead opponents hadn't beaten them in the competition's ultimate showdown since 1904.

Celtic would also be forced to line up without their balletic battering-ram John Hughes on the left wing. The twinkle-toed powerhouse had been getting twice-daily treatments on a leg injury during the week leading up to the grand finale, but had failed a late fitness test. Harry Hood, a clever, ball-playing forward bought from Clyde for a club record £40,000 the previous month, was unavailable as he was Cup-tied following a previous appearance in the competition for the Shawfield outfit.

Stein, on the face of it, looked to have team selection problems. Rangers, too, would be without £100,000 striker

GAME ON...George Connelly and John Hughes prepare for action.

Colin Stein, whose rumbustious, up-and-at-'em approach to the beautiful game had brought a red card too many and his 'reward' would be a seat in the stand that afternoon. Alex Ferguson led the line against Celtic; he wasn't to know it, but it would be his last outing for the club.

It was hardly a secret that Jock Stein enjoyed deploying wingers in his team and Jimmy Johnstone, on the right, and John Hughes, on the opposite flank, had been potent threats that particular season. Now, though, he had to plan for a crucial confrontation without their services. Davie White, the youthful Rangers manager at a mere thirty-five, was ready to pit his tactical wits against his dug-out opponent. He lost big-style.

Stein created a Celtic eleven that would largely ignore raids on the flanks, although, of course, full-backs Jim Craig and Tommy Gemmell would be encouraged to join the attack whenever possible. Connelly was given the No.7 shorts and Bertie Auld, who had kicked off his career as an outside-left, appeared to have been given the opportunity to reprise the role. White, apparently, accepted the dangling carrot.

Neither Connelly nor Auld played as wide Bhoys in the game. Stein manoeuvred the pair into withdrawn midfield roles which flummoxed the Ibrox full-back pairing of Kai Johansen and Willie Mathieson. Without direct opponents to deal with, the defensive duo were enticed further up the field and Stevie Chalmers and Bobby Lennox, two forwards gifted with searing pace, were ordered to expose the space behind Johansen and Mathieson. It was half-time before the confused White could attempt to sort out the mayhem in his defence.

By then, it was a tad too late – Celtic were leading by three clear goals and were well on their way to picking up their twentieth Scottish Cup.

Stein couldn't have wished for a more enterprising start. A corner-kick was claimed on the left-wing and Lennox trotted over to take it, as he had done so many times in the past. His curling delivery eliminated the Ibrox players at the near post and skipper Billy McNeill was generously allowed a clear run at the ball. Majestically, he leapt and, straining his neck muscles to the limit, snapped his head forward, made perfect contact with the sphere and guided a header into keeper Norrie Martin's right-hand corner.

Alex Ferguson had been told to shadow the Celtic captain at set-plays. He was marked absent on this occasion. Afterwards, he was blamed by his Ibrox paymasters for the loss of the crucial goal and his 'crime' was deemed punishable by a lifetime banishment from the Rangers first team. Six months later he joined Falkirk.

With the Rangers back lot still attempting vainly to unravel the conundrum that was presented before them, Celtic took full advantage by scoring two quickfire goals before the half-time whistle. George Connelly was a key player in both strikes. A minute from the interval, he intercepted a ball from Swedish winger Orjan Persson intended for Mathieson. With praiseworthy speed of thought, the youngster diverted a pass to Lennox who enjoyed the freedom of Hampden as he sped through before burying the ball behind the exposed Martin.

Precisely seventy-seven seconds later, Celtic eased to an unassailable three-goal advantage and it was the elegant Connelly who delivered the coup de grace. Martin, possibly still reeling at the loss of the Lennox goal, attempted a short goal-kick to his skipper John Greig, who clearly wasn't expecting the pass. As he tried to bring the ball under control, Connelly sauntered in, took it from him, sidestepped the goalkeeper and rolled a lazy effort into the net. The Celtic end in the 132,870 attendance erupted in joyous bedlam.

It was all over long before Stevie Chalmers, fourteen minutes from time, was invited to utilise the wide, open spaces of the playing field as he ran in unopposed before

Scottish Cup

January 25, 1969: First Round:
PARTICK THISTLE 3 Bone (2), Flanagan
CELTIC 3 Hughes, Wallace, Murdoch

Simpson; Craig, Gemmell; Murdoch, McNeill, Brogan; Johnstone, Callaghan, Wallace, Lennox, Hughes.

January 29: First Round replay:
CELTIC 8 McNeill, Johnstone, Wallace, Callaghan (2), Lennox, Hughes, Gemmell
PARTICK THISTLE 1 Duncan

Simpson; Craig, Gemmell; Murdoch (sub: Chalmers), McNeill, Brogan; Johnstone, Callaghan, Wallace, Lennox, Hughes.

February 12: Second Round:
CLYDE 0
CELTIC 0

Simpson (sub: Auld); Craig, Gemmell; Murdoch, McNeill, Brogan; Johnstone, Lennox, Wallace, Callaghan, Chalmers.

February 24: Second Round replay:
CELTIC 3 Chalmers, Hughes, Murdoch
CLYDE 0

Fallon; Gemmell, O'Neill; Murdoch, McNeill, Hay; Johnstone (sub: Callaghan), Lennox, Wallace, Chalmers, Hughes.

March 5: Third Round:
CELTIC 3 Hughes, Lennox, Chalmers
ST JOHNSTONE 2 Connolly, Hall

Fallon; Craig, Gemmell; Murdoch, McNeill, Clark; Johnstone, Lennox, Wallace, Chalmers, Hughes.

March 22: Semi-final:
CELTIC 4 Wallace, McNeill, Chalmers, Johnstone
MORTON 1 Allan

Fallon; Craig, Gemmell; Murdoch, McNeill, Brogan; Johnstone, Wallace, Chalmers, Auld (sub: Callaghan), Hughes.

April 26: Final:
CELTIC 4 McNeill, Lennox, Connelly, Chalmers
RANGERS 0

Fallon; Craig, Gemmell; Murdoch, McNeill, Brogan; Connelly, Wallace, Chalmers, Auld, Lennox.

lobbing the ball over the right shoulder of the transfixed Martin.

Bertie Auld exclaimed afterwards: "I saw that performance from us twice; once today on the Hampden pitch and once on the manager's tactics board yesterday." Mischievously, he added: "You could say everything went according to plan."

Fallon; Craig, Gemmell; Murdoch, McNeill, Brogan; Connelly, Wallace, Chalmers, Auld and Lennox. ■

Martin O'Neill *profile*

It's an absolute honour for me to be the manager here, I'm telling you that now. It's an absolute honour.

WITHOUT blinking, Martin O'Neill looked at his would-be inquisitors and declared: "Just to be absolutely sure about this, I want you all to know that I bear a grudge. No, I'm not joking. Seriously, I do bear grudges. Honestly, I do."

The new Celtic manager had put down a marker without a ball being kicked in anger.

I was part of the media scrum who had been invited to meet the Irishman at the Crutherland Hotel, nestling amid a gorgeous riot of assorted colours in gardens on the way to East Kilbride, on a gloriously sunny afternoon in June 2000.

About twenty other sports journalists had been given the opportunity to meet and greet the incoming team boss for the first time.

O'Neill had just handed in his notice at Leicester City and was addressing a dining room packed with strangers.

I sat opposite him for an hour or so that day and got the drift he was not an individual who embraced mirth with effortless ease. As a matter of fact, the man who was following in the footsteps of the legendary Jock Stein appeared to be solemn and withdrawn and made little effort to indulge in idle chit-chat.

When it came to coffee and liqueurs, the team boss given the urgent task of breathing life into a team that had been knocked out of the Scottish Cup by Inverness Caley Thistle the previous season moved to the top of the table to grab everyone's attention.

He went through the usual preamble; "Big club, big job, big test." Once he had got the formalities out of the way, the real Martin O'Neill took over and he had no intention of leaving anyone in that room in any shadow of doubt about what he expected in the coming years while he was manager of "one of the greatest football clubs in the world".

He wasn't just talking about his players, either. No member of the press left the Crutherland Hotel that day

FLOATING ON AIR... Martin O'Neill has that uplifting feeling as he celebrates another Celtic goal in their 6-2 thrashing of Rangers in his Old Firm debut.

Scottish Premier League Table

P	Team	Pld	W	D	L	GF	GA	GD	Pts
1	**Celtic**	**38**	**31**	**4**	**3**	**90**	**29**	**+61**	**97**
2	Rangers	38	26	4	8	76	36	+40	82
3	Hibernian	38	18	12	8	57	35	+22	66
4	Kilmarnock	38	15	9	14	44	53	−9	54
5	Hearts	38	14	10	14	56	50	+6	52
6	Dundee	38	13	8	17	51	49	+2	47
7	Aberdeen	38	11	12	15	45	52	−7	45
8	Motherwell	38	12	7	19	42	56	−14	43
9	Dunfermline Athletic	38	11	9	18	34	54	−20	42
10	St Johnstone	38	9	13	16	40	56	−16	40
11	Dundee United	38	9	8	21	38	63	−25	35
12	St Mirren	38	8	6	24	32	72	−40	30

League Cup Final

March 18, 2001: **CELTIC 3** Larsson (3)
KILMARNOCK 0

Gould; Mjallby, Vega, Valgaeren; Healy, Lambert, Lennon, Moravcik (sub: Smith), Petta (sub: Crainey; sub: Boyd); Larsson and Sutton.

Scottish Cup Final

May 26, 2001: **CELTIC 3** McNamara, Larsson (2,1 pen)
HIBS 0

Douglas; Mjallby, Vega, Valgaeren; Agathe, Lambert (sub: Boyd), Lennon, Moravcik (sub: McNamara), Thompson (sub: Johnson); Larsson, Sutton.

BHOYS

CELTIC overcame Rangers 3-1 in an explosive League Cup semi-final at Hampden in February, 2001. The Ibrox side's Claudio Reyna and Michael Mols and Celtic substitute Lubomir Moravcik were red-carded in a melee minutes from the end. Henrik Larsson (2) and Chris Sutton scored the goals with Jorg Albertz replying.

ZONE

with any uncertainty about what to expect from the latest incumbent of the Parkhead dug-out.

"Cross me and you're in trouble." It was loud and clear. Celtic had just appointed a single-minded, fiercely-committed individual who would stand or fall by his harshest decisions.

O'Neill, of course, answered an SOS from Celtic that summer. The previous year's experiment with John Barnes as a rookie manager and Kenny Dalglish as Director of Football Operations had gone catastrophically wrong. The partnership looked good on paper, but, unfortunately, didn't transfer to where it mattered most – the football pitch.

The catalyst was the pulverising defeat from the Highlanders in the Scottish Cup on a raw, piercing evening in the east end of Glasgow when Barnes lost control of his team as they toppled to one of the most embarrassing results in the club's history. There was turmoil in the dressing room at half-time with Celtic trailing 2-1.

Mark Viduka, the club's Australian striker, in the midst of an extravagant temper tantrum, removed his boots and threw them across the dressing room. The shirt followed the footwear moments later. He had no intention of taking any further part in the shambles.

Barnes – with Dalglish out of the country – looked for support. There was none. English veteran forward Ian Wright took Viduka's place for the second-half and the rest, as they say, is history. The Highlanders, thought to be there to simply make up the numbers, added a third goal in their wondrous 3-1 success.

A couple of days later, Barnes was sacked. He had arrived in June 1999 and left in February 2000, heading for managerial oblivion. Dalglish took charge of the team until the end of the campaign and, remarkably, led them to a League Cup triumph, beating Aberdeen 2-0 in the Final.

The Parkhead men actually claimed runners-up spot in the Premier League, a landslide twenty-one points adrift of Rangers, who, unchallenged, cantered to their eleventh title success in twelve years.

Dalglish still had 12 months to run on a contract worth around £600,000 per year. His days were numbered,

TWO CELTIC GREATS... Tommy Burns and Martin O'Neill talk things over.

though, when O'Neill was offered the manager's job. There was not the remotest possibility of O'Neill and Dalglish working together. Dalglish would eventually take the club to the Court of Session in Edinburgh accusing them of unfair dismissal. Figures ranging from £750,000 to £1.2million were bandied about before the sorry, messy situation was settled.

Another problem had to be resolved, too. There was the small matter of O'Neill having already agreed a three-year extension to his Leicester City deal in June 1999, reputedly worth £600,000 a year, matching Dalglish's salary at Parkhead.

By the summer of 2000, O'Neill had been team boss of the West Midlands outfit for five years following his dug-out debut with non-league Wycombe Wanderers in 1990 and moving on for a brief stint at Norwich City in June 1995. The headstrong character from the village of Kilrea, in Northern Ireland, had a disagreement with chairman Robert Chase over transfer policy and resigned six months later.

He joined Leicester immediately after leaving the East Anglian club. He guided the team – then based at Filbert Street with a ground capacity of 22,000 – to the Premier League in his first season. He also led the side to two League Cup Final successes and it wasn't long before clubs with superior financial resources were looking in his direction. O'Neill, bright and astute, triggered his release from his Leicester City contract after exercising a clause that allowed him, during the close season, to speak to clubs interested in obtaining his services. Celtic acted in haste to take up that option.

And, so, on a particularly wet afternoon in the east end of Glasgow, O'Neill, unfalteringly, made his way to the dias at the front door at Celtic Park on the unseasonal first day of June and, holding up his left hand to acknowledge the cheers of his new admirers, he had a few words for the gathering throng.

O'Neill said: "First of all, thank you very much for waiting in the rain. I really appreciate it." He paused, waved again and continued: "It's an absolute honour for me to be the manager here, I'm telling you that now. It's an absolute

SILVERWARE CLEAN SWEEP...Martin O'Neill with the Scottish Cup, Premier League championship and League Cup – all won in his first season as Celtic manager.

RAGING CALM...Martin O'Neill and celebrating Neil Lennon, Alan Thompson and Didier Agathe after the 3-0 Scottish Cup Final success over Hibs.

LIP SERVICE...Martin O'Neill looks a little tongue-tied as he holds the Scottish Cup.

IT'S OURS...Paul Lambert and Tommy Boyd share the applause as they are presented with the silverware.

honour." He stepped back as the rapturous applause gathered momentum.

He signed off: "I will do everything I possibly can to bring some success here to the football club. Thank you." And with that the fourteenth full-time manager in Celtic history disappeared back into the labyrinth of his new football home where he would rule for five extremely interesting years.

O'Neill would be working again with John Robertson, his former Nottingham Forest team-mate who was also his assistant at Wycombe, Norwich and Leicester, and Steve Walford, his Head Coach at Carrow Road and Filbert Street. O'Neill extended Tommy Burns' emergency contract from the previous season to coach alongside Walford. Burns didn't need any persuading to agree the deal.

You better believe O'Neill would have had the inside track of the histrionics in the home dressing room during the shameful evening of the Caley Thistle debacle.

The intransigent Viduka had made noises about wanting to move and he got his wish when he was transferred swiftly to Leeds United for £6million and the new Celtic manager quickly passed that same amount of cash to Chelsea for Chris Sutton, a direct and more robust replacement for the man from Down Under, who could often mix brilliance with belligerence.

Sutton became an instant hero with the Parkhead faithful. After completing the signing, he said: "I know the expectations of the Celtic fans. That's to win the league and put Rangers in their place." Sharp and succinct, the words of a winner.

O'Neill, with the backing of major shareholder Dermot Desmond, wasn't hanging about in the transfer market as he strengthened his inherited squad. He didn't hesitate in parting with £3.8million to Dutch outfit Roda for Belgian international defender Joos Valgaeren.

Astute left-sided midfielder Alan Thompson arrived in a £2.75million deal from Aston Villa while French winger Didier Agathe, dubbed the Bhoy Racer for obvious reasons as he scorched up and down the touchline, was brought in for a nominal £200,000 from Hibs where he was coming to the end of his short-term deal with the Easter Road club.

In October, Dundee keeper Rab Douglas agreed a £1.2million switch to Parkhead – knocking back interest from Rangers in the process – and O'Neill finally landed his Leicester City protege Neil Lennon in December for £6million after months of tracking his former skipper.

While he was putting his squad together, there were a few who did not impress O'Neill, one being expensive defender Rafael Scheidt who had arrived in Scotland on a reported £4.5million transfer fee from South American outfit Gremio.

O'Neill made his mind up about the bungling Brazilian after only a few minutes of seeing him in action in a pre-season game in Ireland, a 3-2 win over Bray Wanderers. The centre-half, with time and space, elected to shell a ball down the wing and, in doing so, almost decapitated the new Celtic boss who had to swiftly duck as the hurtling object sizzled over his head and into the unfortunate fans behind the dug-out.

A loan deal was put in place post-haste to take Scheidt back to Brazil with Corinthians for a year. The player had an interesting take on his days in Glasgow. He told South American journalists: "I have left the hell that has been unbearable for me. I have suffered a massive process of rejection. Football is ping-pong with the ball going back and forward. Martin O'Neill has told me he thinks I am not good enough to play for Celtic. He told me to tackle harder, to fight for every single ball and to elbow my opponents. I told him I couldn't do that and he thought I never followed his instructions."

O'Neill later admitted to being "completely baffled" at the thought of anyone spending any amount of cash on the only Brazilian player he had ever witnessed who couldn't control and pass the ball. The defender's temporary transfer with Corinthians was extended for a further season and he said he wanted to return to Celtic after that period to show his real qualities.

Choosing his words as carefully as he picked his passes, the South American was quoted as saying: "I want the year to be known as the Scheidt year".

Thankfully, Martin O'Neill's debut season was a lot more memorable. ▪

HAIL! HAIL! Martin O'Neill salutes the supporters.

BHOYS

CHRIS SUTTON cost Chelsea £10 million when they signed him from Blackburn Rovers in 1999. Remarkably, he managed to score just one league goal – in a 5-0 win over Manchester United – before moving to Celtic a year later.

ZONE

BHOY OH, BHOY...Chris Sutton and Lubomir Moravcik celebrate a strike against Rangers with unconfined delight.

Six of the Best

DUNDEE UNITED 1
CELTIC 2
(July 30, 2000)

YOU only get one opportunity to make a first impression – and Martin O'Neill's expertise in the timing department didn't desert him during his competitive introduction to life as Celtic's new manager.

The Irishman took his bow in front of a frenzied 11,761 supporters at a noisy Tannadice on a radiant Sunday evening in summer. The sun shone as his players, adorned in their gold shirts, took the field with two of O'Neill's initial line-up making their debuts for the club, defender Joos Valgaeren and striker Chris Sutton, who had arrived at Parkhead for a combined £9.8million in transfer fees.

Like O'Neill, the Belgian and the Englishman seized upon the chance to insinuate themselves with their new followers. One thing which was abundantly clear from the onset of this confrontation was that the Parkhead performers had found again the commitment and desire that had been absent under the previous regime. O'Neill's man-management skills were one of the main components in the team boss' successful reign at Leicester City.

It took Celtic until eight minutes before the interval to get their reward against a tenacious Tayside outfit who were determined to pull the red carpet from under their newly-charged opponents who had a lot to prove following an embarrassing campaign that had seen them finish twenty-one points adrift of Rangers in the league.

Paul Lambert and Sutton were involved in the build-up before the ball broke to the ever-reliable Henrik Larsson and he almost casually swept a first-time left-foot effort from sixteen yards beyond the diving Alan Combe for the first goal in the Martin O'Neill era.

Four minutes after the turnaround, though, Dundee United were invited back into proceedings when they were presented with an equaliser. Neil Heaney curled over a left-wing free-kick and keeper Jonathan Gould collided with Jackie McNamara as he attempted to deal with the cross. David McCracken was left with a vacant goal in front of him

DREADLOCK HAPPY BHOY... Henrik Larsson in typical pose after a Celtic goal against old foes Rangers.

and he keenly accepted the invite to thump a header into the net.

Under John Barnes and Kenny Dalglish the preceding season, the players' spirits may have nosedived. This, however, was a different Celtic. They met the challenge square-on and, in the sixty-sixth minute, fought their way to the winning goal. McNamara saw a vicious drive pushed away by the sprawling Combe. The ball rebounded to French defender Stephane Mahe and he whipped in a low cross to the back post where debutant Sutton raced in to blast the ball into the net. Celtic were on their way to a magical season.

Gould; Boyd, Stubbs, Valgaeren, Mahe; McNamara, Lambert, Berkovic (sub: Johnson), Petrov; Larsson, Sutton.

NEIL LENNON...
midfield enforcer.

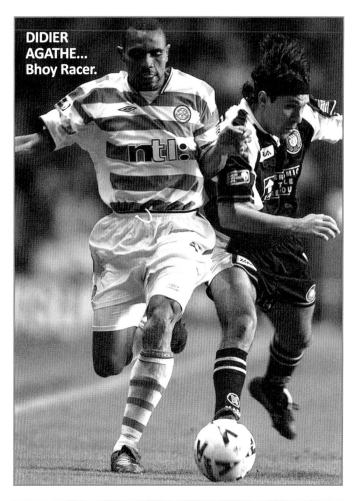

DIDIER AGATHE...
Bhoy Racer.

PAUL LAMBERT...
class act.

JACKIE McNAMARA...
driving force.

HENRIK LARSSON scored five goals in the two domestic Cup Finals – three in the 3-0 win over Kilmarnock in the League Cup and two in the 3-0 triumph against Hibs in the Scottish Cup.

ECSTASY...Henrik Larsson turns away after scoring once more against Rangers with Joos Valgaren behind him. Agony for dejected Ibrox midfielder Giovanni van Bronckhorst.

CELTIC 6
RANGERS 2
(August 27, 2000)

IT WAS dubbed the Demolition Derby. It was the day Martin O'Neill's renascent Celtic team exploded out of the shadows of their age-old rivals and proved they would not be the walkover they had been for the previous twelve months.

It took Chris Sutton a mere fifty-one seconds to give the home side the advantage in a gleefully lop-sided encounter that saw the Ibrox team mercilessly and ruthlessly exposed while being demolished by a well-primed unit.

The first goal arrived before the confrontation had ticked beyond a minute. Lubomir Moravcik, the little Slovakian sorceror, sent in a left-wing corner that was knocked down by Alan Stubbs. Henrik Larsson – of all people! – miscued smack in front of goal and the ball ran on to Sutton, lurking with intent at the far post, and the striker rammed the ball home from two yards. The party had started early. Astoundingly, Celtic were three goals to the good by the eleventh minute.

Another deadball effort from Moravcik caught the Rangers defence doing a fair imitation of exhibits at Madame Tussaud's and Stiliyan Petrov raced in unattended to throw himself at the ball to fire a header past the dumbfounded Stefan Klos. With the Celtic fans going crazy with joy, Paul Lambert came onto a Moravcik pass to blast number three into the net. It was bedlam at Celtic Park as manager O'Neill bounced up and down the touchline.

There was a temporary reprieve for the visitors when Claudio Reyna pulled one back with a header at the back post five minutes from the turnaround. In the fiftieth minute, Larsson scored one of his memorable goals for Celtic. Jonathan Gould punted the ball downfield and it was knocked to the Swede by Sutton. The svelte frontman took the pass in his stride, completely bamboozled Bert Konterman with some nifty footwork and then audaciously chipped the flapping Klos from the edge of the penalty area.

Five minutes later, with the action simply pulsating, Billy Dodds slotted in a penalty-kick, but it was negated again by Larsson as he rose to a Bobby Petta free-kick to glance a header into the keeper's top right-hand corner. With a minute to go, Stephane Mahe flashed over a cross from the left and Sutton finished what he had started by sliding in to touch the ball over the line for number six.

Amid the chaos and the carnage suffered by the Ibrox side, manager Dick Advocaat said sportingly: "Quite simply, we have to give the credit to Celtic. The scoreline doesn't lie and they deserved to win."

Gould; Stubbs, Valgaeren, Mahe; McNamara, Petrov, Lambert (sub: Mjallby), Moravcik (sub: Boyd), Petta; Larsson (sub: Burchill), Sutton.

DUNDEE 1
CELTIC 2
(December 10, 2000)

NEIL LENNON, a future captain and manager of Celtic, made his debut for the club on a freezing Sunday evening on Tayside shortly after his £6million arrival from Leicester City.

The Northern Ireland international midfielder had rejected the offer of a new deal with the English side to team up again with mentor Martin O'Neill at Parkhead. He swiftly realised what he could expect during his years with his boyhood favourites against an exciting Dundee team, heavily laced with colourful Latins and managed by eccentric Italian Ivano Bonetti. Former Argentina World Cup winner Claudio Caniggia was a main protagonist in Dark Blue during an eventful ninety minutes.

Celtic started and finished well, but, in between, great credit must be given to a line-up that made life distinctly uncomfortable for the the visitors. In took Martin O'Neill's team only four minutes to snatch the initiative when Didier Agathe, a bargain buy from Hibs, kicked off the move with a probing run down the right touchline. His long crossfield pass was gathered by Lubomir Moravcik who, in turn, switched it inside to Stiliyan Petrov. The Bulgarian carried it on before blasting past the exposed Marco Roccati.

Bonetti's men were stung into instant retaliation and the Celtic defence, stubbornly marshalled by Johan Mjallby and Joos Valgaeren in front of ex-Dens goalie Rab Douglas, held out until the fifty-fifth minute when they were undone by team-mate Tommy Boyd. Caniggia, who had been performing supremely on the left wing, raced free once more to launch a low ball across the face of goal. Juan Sara was about to throw himself at the inviting ball, but Boyd beat him to it and to his horror his clearance flew straight into the back of his own net.

Dundee had the bulk of play as they sought the winner, but, in the fading moments, O'Neill's team staged a classic smash-and-grab act. Petrov swung in a corner-kick, Mjallby got his head to it, the ball bounced on the six-yard line, Rocatti failed to gather and Agathe appeared at the far post to stab the ball home. Welcome to Scottish football, Mr Lennon!

Douglas; Boyd, Mjallby, Valgaeren; Agathe, Petrov, Lennon, Thompson, Petta (sub: McNamara); Larsson, Moravcik (sub: Johnson).

RAB DOUGLAS, Celtic's £1.2million goalkeeper, missed the 2000/01 League Cup Final victory as he had played in the competition in an earlier round with Dundee. Jonathan Gould deputised. Douglas returned for the Scottish Cup win.

CELTIC 1
RANGERS 0
(February 11, 2001)

THE heavens opened and Paradise beckoned. Celtic went into this rain-lashed encounter in the knowledge a win would give them a twelve-point advantage over their Ibrox rivals at a vitally important stage of the campaign.

on Tommy Boyd and invite him to take no further part in the proceedings. Celtic were already a goal ahead by this stage Although arguably it should have been a two-goal advantage.

In the eighth minute, Swiss defender Ramon Vega, who joined on loan from Spurs the previous month, nodded in a corner-kick from a Thompson deadball delivery. It looked a legitimate goal, but the match official ruled it out for reasons only known to himself. TV pictures later proved Vega had done nothing wrong in the execution of his header.

Martin O'Neill's men, however, had better fortune in the sixteenth minute when they claimed the winner. The hapless Ricksen literally had a hand in the only goal of the game.

BHOYS ZONE

ALAN THOMPSON scored seven goals against Rangers in his seven years at the Hoops. He was also sent off three times against the Ibrox side!

READY FOR TAKE-OFF...Alan Thompson prepares for celebrations after scoring the crucial winner against Rangers.

Equally, Dick Advocaat realised his team had the opportunity to claw back three big points from the Parkhead outfit's lead before they disappeared out of sight. The sodden conditions didn't interrupt another hell-for-leather meeting of the Glasgow giants as they went for each other's jugular.

It was all too much for visiting defender Fernando Ricksen who didn't last the entirety of the first-half. The Dutch right-back, who had been taken off after only twenty-one minutes of his team's 6-2 thrashing at the same ground in August, didn't give his manager the opportunity to substitute him on this frenzied occasion.

He was booked early on for a foul on Alan Thompson and left referee Hugh Dallas with no option but to book him again in the forty-fourth minute for a nonsensical challenge

He dithered so long in taking a throw-in that referee Dallas awarded the shy to Celtic. With his team-mates out of position, Boyd took it quickly to Henrik Larsson who played a neat one-two with strike partner Chris Sutton before setting up Thompson. The midfielder raced forward and prodded the ball left-footed away from Stefan Klos.

Disappointed Ibrox boss Dick Advocaat said reasonably at the end: "We have to be realistic. It's now going to be very difficult to catch Celtic."

He got that right.

Douglas; Mjallby (sub: Tebily), Vega, Boyd; Agathe, Lambert, Lennon, Thompson, Petta; Larsson, Sutton.

YOU BEAUTY...Bulgarian ace Stiliyan Petrov turns away after scoring with a flying header against Rangers. Ibrox defender Lorenzo Amoruso doesn't share his delight.

BHOYS ZONE

JOHN BARNES paid £2.8million to Bulgarian outfit CSKA Sofia for young midfielder Stiliyan Petrov in 1999. Kenny Dalglish, the Director of Football Operations, sanctioned the bargain move for a player who became a firm favourite with the Celtic support. He later rejoined Martin O'Neill at Aston Villa for £6million in 2006.

CELTIC 1
ST MIRREN 0
(April 7, 2001)

THE historic goal didn't quite match the occasion. A crowd of 60,440 – the biggest in Scotland throughout the season – turned out to see if Celtic could clinch the title in Martin O'Neill's debut season in charge.

There were five games still to go when the Paisley outfit, without an away success throughout the campaign, turned up in the east end of Glasgow in the hopes of postponing Flag Day and the crowning of new champions. Some hope!

Johan Mjallby and Alan Thompson hit the woodwork, Henrik Larsson proved he was human by fluffing his final effort with just keeper Ludovic Roy to beat and a variety of other efforts flew high and wide. It was left to Tommy Johnson to snatch the glory goal seven minutes from the interval.

CELTIC won the title with a total of ninety-seven points from thirty-eight games. They were fifteen points better off than runners-up Rangers.

With an anxiety-riddled rearguard backing off, Larsson danced his way into the danger zone before pushing a pass in front of the unmarked Johnson. The fans groaned in unison, though, as the former Aston Villa and Derby County forward took an awful first touch. However, he managed to regain his composure before sliding the ball goalwards.

Frenchman Roy looked surprised, possibly believing the opportunity had been lost, and the effort rolled into the net. It wasn't a classic and it wouldn't be rerun in TV sports programmes for years to come, but that didn't matter to the home support. They almost lifted the roofs of the stands with their delerious yells of unconfined joy.

It was Celtic's thirty-seventh championship triumph and it was made special because of O'Neill's presence. He had invested wisely in bringing players such as Chris Sutton, Alan Thompson, Neil Lennon, Joos Valgaeren, Didier Agathe and Rab Douglas to the club. Ramon Vega arrived at the right time on loan from Spurs, but returned to the London outfit in the summer. The new manager had to be complimented, too, with the work he had done with left-winger Bobby Petta who had been rejuvenated with the arrival of the Irishman.

The handsome league championship trophy was returning to Parkhead, but O'Neill knew there was the little matter of a Scottish Cup to be won to keep it and the League Cup company.

Douglas; Mjallby, Vega, Valgaeren (sub: Boyd); Agathe, Lambert, Lennon, Moravcik (sub: Healy), Thompson; Larsson, Johnson (sub: McNamara).

RANGERS 0
CELTIC 3
(April 29, 2001)

DELIGHT abounded in Govan as Henrik Larsson scored his fiftieth goal of a spectacular season, Lubomir Moravcik claimed two excellent solo efforts, Martin O'Neill's team beat Rangers for the fourth time in five meetings and Celtic, newly-crowned champions, tasted success at Ibrox for the first time in seven years.

There was a carnival atmosphere among the visiting support who had seen their favourites emphatically beaten by four clear goals in their past two visits – 5-1 in November during this campaign and 4-0 thirteen months beforehand. The turnaround in fortunes between two of world football's biggest adversaries was nothing short of incredible. Fact, indeed, can be stranger than fiction.

There was the usual sparring between Scotland's two heayweights before the deadlock was broken in the sixty-first minute. A swift free-kick from Neil Lennon released Larsson and the Swede underlined his wonderful vision with a deft touch inside to set Moravcik running free. The Slovakian dodged past Bert Konterman and made a beeline for goal before the opposing defenders could grasp the situation. Moravcik carried on, Lorenzo Amoruso was too slow and ponderous to close him down and he rifled an effort wide of Stefan Klos.

The cheers were still ringing around the Celtic end when Moravcik repeated the feat in the seventy-fourth minute. This time Rab Douglas cleared a ball downfield to seventeen-year-old Shaun Maloney, making his first appearance as a substitute for Tommy Johnson, and he nudged it in front of his veteran team-mate.

Moravcik showed a surprising burst of speed as he raced away from Fernando Ricksen and once again carried the ball into the box before cleverly clipping it wide of Klos who had anticipated a shot going across him to his left. Little Lubo rarely did the expected.

With four minutes remaining, the goal everyone had been waiting for arrived – Henrik's half-century. Jackie McNamara robbed the dithering Turkish midfielder Tugay on the Celtic left. He knocked a pass into space behind the Ibrox defence and Larsson, with his usual keen anticipation, latched onto the ball, waltzed away from the outrushing Klos and stroked the ball into the vacant net with his left foot.

Could life as a Celtic supporter get any sweeter? On May 26 the Parkhead followers would get their answer when they took on Alex McLeish's talented Hibs side in the Scottish Cup Final at a sun-drenched Hampden.

Douglas; Mjallby, Vega, Valgaeren; Agathe, Lambert (sub: Boyd), Lennon, Moravcik (sub: McNamara), Thompson; Larsson, Johnson (sub: Maloney). ■

HANDS UP...if you've scored fifty goals! Henrik Larsson celebrates with Joos Valgaeren and Alan Thompson after hitting the half-century against Rangers.

BHOYS ZONE

HENRIK LARSSON scored his fiftieth goal of the season in the final Old Firm game – a 3-0 win over Rangers at Ibrox in April. Lubomir Moravcik claimed the other two.

Scottish Premier League Results

July 30, 2000: **DUNDEE UNITED 1** McCracken
CELTIC 2 Larsson, Sutton

Gould; Boyd, Stubbs, Valgaeren, Mahe; McNamara, Petrov, Lambert, Berkovic (sub: Johnson); Larsson, Sutton.

August 5: **CELTIC 1** Petrov
MOTHERWELL 0

Gould; Boyd, Tebily, Valgaeren, Mahe: McNamara, Petrov, Lambert, Berkovic (sub: Mjallby); Larsson, Sutton.

August 13: **CELTIC 2** Larsson, Johnson
KILMARNOCK 1 McLaren

Gould; Boyd (sub: Mjallby), Stubbs, Valgaeren, Mahe; Petrov, Lambert, Moravcik, Petta; Larsson, Johnson.

August 19: **HEARTS 2** Severin, Juanjo
CELTIC 4 Sutton (2), Larsson, Moravcik

Gould; Stubbs (sub: Mjallby), Valgaeren, Mahe; McNamara, Petrov, Lambert, Moravcik (sub: Boyd), Petta; Larsson, Sutton.

August 27: **CELTIC 6** Sutton (2), Larsson (2), Petrov, Lambert
RANGERS 2 Reyna, Dodds (pen)

Gould; Stubbs, Valgaeren, Mahe; McNamara, Petrov, Lambert (sub: Mjallby), Moravcik (sub: Boyd), Petta; Larsson, Sutton.

September 9: **CELTIC 3** Larsson (2, 1pen), Burchill
HIBS 0

Gould; Boyd, Stubbs (sub: Mjallby), Valgaeren; McNamara, Petrov, Lambert, Moarvcik (sub: Burchill), Thompson' Larsson, Sutton.

September 18: **DUNFERMLINE 1** Crawford (pen)
CELTIC 2 Larsson (2, 1 pen)

Gould; Boyd, Valgaeren, Mahe (sub: Moravcik); McNamara, Petrov, Lambert, Mjallby, Thompson; Larsson, Sutton.

September 23: **CELTIC 1** Petrov
DUNDEE 0

Gould; Boyd, Mjallby, Valgaeren; McNamara, Petrov, Lambert, Moravcik (sub: Stubbs), Thompson (sub: Healy); Larsson, Sutton.

October 1: **ABERDEEN 1** Winters
CELTIC 1 Larsson

Gould; Boyd, Mjallby, Valgaeren; McNamara, Petrov, Lambert (sub: Moravcik), Thompson (sub: Mahe; sub: Healy), Petta; Larsson, Sutton.

October 14: **CELTIC 2** Sutton, Larsson
ST MIRREN 0

Gould; Boyd, Mjallby, Valgaeren; Agathe, Petrov (sub: Healy), Lambert, Moravcik (sub: Riseth), Thompson; Larsson, Sutton.

October 17: **ST JOHNSTONE 0**
CELTIC 2 Larsson (pen), Valgaeren

Gould; Boyd, Mjallby, Valgaeren; Agathe, Petrov (sub: Healy), Lambert, Thompson, Petta; Larsson, Sutton.

October 21: **CELTIC 2** Larsson, Thompson
DUNDEE UNITED 1 Lambert (og)

Gould; Boyd, Mjallby, Valgaeren; Agathe, Petrov, Lambert, Thompson, Petta (sub: McNamara); Larsson, Sutton.

October 29: **MOTHERWELL 3** Adams, McCulloch, Brannan (pen)
CELTIC 3 Mjallby, Valgaeren, McNamara

Gould; Boyd, Mjallby, (sub: Stubbs), Valgaeren; McNamara, Petrov, Lambert, Thompson, Petta; Agathe (sub: Moravcik), Larsson.

November 5: **KILMARNOCK 0**
CELTIC 1 Thompson

Gould; Boyd, Mjallby, Valgaeren; McNamara, Petrov (sub: Healy), Lambert, Thompson, Petta; Larsson, Sutton.

November 12: **CELTIC 4** Sutton, Larsson (2), Moravcik
ST JOHNSTONE 1 Russell

Douglas; Mjallby, Stubbs, Valgaeren; Agathe, Petrov (sub: Healy), Moravcik, Thompson, Petta; Larsson (sub: Berkovic), Sutton (sub: Johnson).

November 18: **CELTIC 6** Valgaeren, Moravcik, Larsson (2), Mjallby, Petrov
HEARTS 1 Cameron

Douglas; Boyd, Mjallby (sub: Tebily), Valgaeren; Agathe, Petrov, Moravcik (sub: McNamara), Thompson, Petta; Larsson, Sutton (sub: Johnson).

November 26: **RANGERS 5** Ferguson, Flo, De Boer, Amoruso, Mols
CELTIC 1 Larsson

Douglas; Boyd, Mjallby (sub: Mahe), Valgaeren; Agathe, Petrov. Moravcik (sub: McNamara), Thompson, Petta; Larsson, Sutton (sub: Johnson).

November 29: **HIBS 0**
CELTIC 0

Douglas; Boyd, Mjallby, Valgaeren; Agathe, McNamara, Petrov, Healy (sub: Moravcik), Petta (sub: Mahe); Larsson, Sutton.

December 2: **CELTIC 3** Moravcik, Larsson, Johnson
DUNFERMLINE 1 Dair

Douglas; Boyd, Mjallby, Valgaren; Agathe, Petrov, Moravcik (sub: McNamara), Thompson, Petta: Larsson, Johnson.

December 10: **DUNDEE 1** Boyd (og)
CELTIC 2 Petrov, Agathe

Douglas; Boyd, Mjallby, Valgaeren; Agathe, Petrov, Lennon, Thompson, Petta (sub: McNamara); Larsson, Moravcik (sub: Johnson).

December 16: **CELTIC 6** Larsson (3), Vega (2), Smith
ABERDEEN 0

Douglas; Mjallby, Vega, Valgaeren; Agathe (sub: Smith), Petrov, Lennon, Thompson, Petta (sub: McNamara); Larsson, Johnson.

December 23: **ST MIRREN 0**
CELTIC 2 Agathe, Larsson

Douglas; Mjallby, Vega, Valgaeren; Agathe, Petrov, Lennon, Thompson, Petta (sub: McNamara); Larsson, Sutton.

December 26: **DUNDEE UNITED 0**
CELTIC 4 Larsson (pen), Sutton (2), Petrov

Douglas; Mjallby, Vega, Valgaeren; Agathe, McNamara, Petrov (sub: Johnson), Lennon, Petta (sub: Smith); Larsson (sub: Moravcik), Sutton.

January 2, 2001: **CELTIC 6** Sutton (2), Larsson (4)
KILMARNOCK 0

Douglas; Mjallby, Vega, Valgaeren; Agathe, McNamara (sub: Smith), Petrov (sub: Moravcik), Lennon, Petta (sub: Thompson); Larsson, Sutton.

February 4: **HEARTS 0**
CELTIC 3 Larsson (3)

Douglas; Mjallby, Vega, Valgaeren (sub: Boyd); Agathe, McNamara, Lambert, Lennon, Thompson (sub: Moravcik), Larsson (sub: Smith), Sutton.

February 11: **CELTIC 1** Thompson
RANGERS 0

Douglas; Mjallby (sub: Tebily), Vega, Boyd; Agathe, Lambert, Lennon, Thompson, Petta; Larsson, Sutton.

February 21: **CELTIC 1** Moravcik
MOTHERWELL 0

Douglas; Mjallby, Vega, Valgaeren (sub: Boyd); Agathe, Lambert (sub: Moravcik), Lennon, Thompson, Petta (sub: Petrov); Larsson, Sutton.

February 25: **CELTIC 1** Mjallby
HIBS 1 Libbra

Douglas; Mjallby, Vega, Boyd; Agathe, Petrov, Lambert (sub: Moravcik), Lennon, Thompson; Larsson, Sutton.

March 4: **DUNFERMLINE 0**
CELTIC 3 Petrov, Larsson, Lennon

Douglas; Mjallby, Vega, Valgaeren; Agathe, Petrov, Lambert, Lennon (sub: Crainey), Thompson; Larsson, Sutton (sub: Johnson).

March 14: **ST JOHNSTONE 1** McCluskey
CELTIC 2 Johnson, Larsson

Douglas; Mjallby, Vega, Valgaeren; Agathe (sub: Crainey), Petrov (sub: McNamara), Lambert, Lennon, Thompson; Larsson, Johnson.

April 1: **ABERDEEN 0**
CELTIC 1 Agathe

Douglas; Mjallby, Vega, Valgaeren; Agathe, Healy (sub: McNamara), Lambert, Lennon, Thompson; Larsson, Johnson (sub: Moravcik).

April 4: **CELTIC 2** Johnson, Mjallby
DUNDEE 1 Sara

Douglas; Mjallby, Vega, Valgaeren; Agathe, Lambert, Lennon, Moravcik (sub: Boyd), Thompson; Larsson, Johnson (sub: McNamara).

April 7: **CELTIC 1** Johnson
ST MIRREN 0

Douglas; Mjallby, Vega, Valgaeren (sub: Boyd); Agathe, Lambert, Lennon, Moravcik (sub: Healy), Thompson; Larsson, Johnson (sub: McNamara).

April 22: **CELTIC 1** Moravcik
HEARTS 0

Douglas; Mjallby, Vega, Valgaeren; Agathe, McNamara, Lambert (sub: Boyd), Healy (sub: Moravcik), Thompson; Larsson, Johnson (sub: Smith).

April 29: **RANGERS 0**
CELTIC 3 Moravcik (2), Larsson

Douglas; Mjallby, Vega, Valgaeren; Agathe, Lambert (sub: Boyd), Lennon, Moravcik (sub: McNamara), Thompson; Larsson, Johnson (sub: Maloney).

May 6: **HIBS 2** Libbra (2)
CELTIC 5 McNamara (2), Larsson, Stubbs, Moravcik

Kharine; Boyd, Vega, Valgaeren (sub: Stubbs); Agathe, McNamara, Lambert, Lennon, Thompson; Larsson, Moravcik.

May 13: **CELTIC 0**
DUNDEE 2 Caballero (2)

Gould; Mjallby, Vega (sub: Boyd), Valgaeren (sub: Stubbs); McNamara, Lambert, Lennon, Moravcik, Thompson; Larsson, Smith (sub: Maloney).

May 20: **KILMARNOCK 1** Mahood
CELTIC 0

Douglas; Boyd, Vega, Tebily; McNamara, Stubbs, Healy, Fotheringham, Mahe; Smith, Maloney.

UEFA Cup Results

August 10, 2000: Qualifying Round: 1st leg:
JEUNESSE ESCH 0
CELTIC 4 Moravcik (2), Larsson, Petta

Gould; Mjallby, Vagaeren, Mahe; McNamara (sub: Johnson), Riseth, Lambert, Moravcik, Petta; Larsson (sub: Healy), Sutton.

August 24: 2nd leg:
CELTIC 7 Burchill (3), Berkovic (2), Riseth, Petrov
JEUNESS ESCH 0 (Aggregate: 11-0)

Gould; Mjallby, Scheidt, Tebily; Healy, Riseth, Lambert (sub: Boyd), Berkovic, Petta; Lynch (sub: Petrov), Burchill (sub: Miller).

September 14: First Round: 1st leg:
CELTIC 2 Larsson (2)
HJK HELSINKI 0

Gould; Boyd, Mjallby, Valgaeren; McNamara, Petrov, Lambert, Moravcik (sub: Berkovic), Mahe (sub: Healy); Larsson, Sutton.

September 28: 2nd leg:
HJK HELSINKI 2 Roiha (2)
CELTIC 1 (After extra-time; 2-0 at 90 mins; Aggregate: 3-2) Sutton

Gould; Boyd (sub: Riseth), Mjallby, Valgaeren; McNamara, Petrov (sub: Moravcik), Lambert, Berkovic (sub: Healy), Petta; Larsson, Sutton.

October 26: Second Round: 1st leg:
BORDEUX 1 Dugarry
CELTIC 1 Larsson (pen)

Gould; Boyd, Mjallby, Valgaeren; Agathe, McNamara, Petrov, Lambert, Petta (sub: Healy); Larsson, Moravcik.

November 19: 2nd leg:
CELTIC 1 Moravcik
BORDEUX 2 (After extra-time; 1-1 at 90 mins; Aggregate: 2-3) Laslandes (2)

Gould; Boyd, Mjallby, Valgaeren; Agathe, McNamara (sub: Healy), Petrov, Moravcik (sub: Johnson), Petta (sub: Berkovic); Larsson, Sutton.

Lightning Larsson!

SWEDE DREAMS...Henrik Larsson takes the plaudits of his team-mates again after his stunning League Cup Final hat-trick against Kilmarnock. Lubomir Moravcik, Stephen Crainey, Ramon Vega and Joos Valgaeren share the joy.

CELTIC 3
KILMARNOCK 0
(March 18, 2001)

THERE was no surprise this League Cup triumph was named 'The Larsson Final' following a mesmeric performance from the spellbinding Swedish striker.

The 48,831 spectators at Hampden were simply left in a state of hypnosis as Henrik Larsson magically produced a devastating second-half display of ruthless finishing to flash in a hat-trick to lift his season's goal tally to a remarkable forty-seven while despatching the Ayrshire team to also-ran status.

Kille couldn't say they weren't well warned about the menace of Larsson. Two days into 2001, they were first-foots to Parkhead on league business and were demoralised 6-0 with the elusive marksman claiming four and Chris Sutton adding the two others. The Celtic double-act would sample contrasting fortunes in this Hampden Final.

It was stalemated at the interval with a rugged Killie outfit refusing to give their opponents – especially Larsson – space in which to operate. Their tackling was robust, to say the least, and Bobby Petta's time on the pitch didn't go beyond the tenth minute when he was forced to limp off after a sturdy challenge from Alan Mahood. Substitute Stephen Crainey took the Dutchman's place on the left-hand side of the midfield five.

For most of the opening forty-five minutes, it was raw fare for the fans. No quarter was asked or given by two sets of players with their eye on the prize. At this stage of the campaign, no-one at Celtic was talking about the possibility of the third clean sweep in the club's history. But the players and the club's followers were allowed to dream.

Following the cat-and-mouse tactics of the first-half, it was evident the only way Martin O'Neill's men could entice their opponents out of their defensive shell was to score a goal which would compel them to ditch the safety-first outlook. That man Larsson duly obliged. Only two minutes after the turnaround, Celtic won a corner-kick when Gordon Marshall pushed away a shot from young Colin Healy, playing instead of the suspended Jackie McNamara.

CHRIS SUTTON was Martin O'Neill's first buy for the club, arriving for £6million from Chelsea in the summer of 2000. He scored on his debut, a 2-1 win over Dundee United at Tannadice on the opening day of the season.

A short one was touched to Lubomir Moravcik on the right and he curled over an inviting cross. Ramon Vega diverted the ball to Larsson and he had to readjust his body shape in an instant as he acrobatically volleyed a close-range effort into the net.

Celtic fans waited for the floodgates to open, but there was a moment of high drama when Sutton was issued with a straight red card by referee Hugh Dallas following a challenge on Gary Holt. It looked harsh and O'Neill, after watching the incident again on TV monitors at the ground, was disinclined to agree with the match official's judgement and observed: "A yellow card might have been enough."

In the seventy-fourth minute, Larsson sparked to life again. Moravcik spotted his team-mate racing free on the right and picked him out with an impeccable through pass. Larsson summed up the situation in a heartbeat and stroked the ball towards goal from an angle. It took a touch off frantic defender Chris Innes and spun high over the head of keeper Marshall.

Nine minutes from time, the Swede sprinkled some more stardust over the proceedings. Picking up the ball a few yards inside Killie's half, he simply darted towards Marshall's goal. Kevin Gowne was left in his slipstream as Larsson zeroed in on his quarry. Anxiously, the Rugby Park No.1 left his goal only to be left in an undignified heap as the masterly Celt

League Cup

September 5, 2000:

First Round:
CELTIC 4 Sutton, Johnson (2,1 pen), Thompson
RAITH ROVERS 0

Kerr; Boyd, Valgaeren, Mahe; McNamara, Healy, Thompson, Petta (sub: Tebily; sub: Scheidt); Johnson, Sutton, Burchill.

November 1: Quarter-Final:
HEARTS 2 Cameron (2 pens)
CELTIC 5 (After extra-time; 2-2 at 90 mins) Crainey, Smith, Healy, Moravcik, McNamara

Gould; Riseth, Stubbs, Valgaeren; McNamara, Healy, Moravcik, Crainey (sub: Petta), Thompson; Smith (sub: Petrov), Johnson (sub: Boyd).

February 7, 2001: Semi-Final:
CELTIC 3 Sutton, Larsson (2,1 pen)
RANGERS 1 Albertz (pen)

Gould; Mjallby, Vega, Boyd (sub: Johnson); McNamara (sub: Petta), Petrov, Lambert, Lennon, Thompson; Larsson (sub: Moravcik), Sutton.

March 18: Final:
CELTIC 3 Larsson (3)
KILMARNOCK 0

Gould; Mjallby, Vega, Valgaeren; Healy, Lambert, Lennon, Moravcik (sub: Smith), Petta (sub: Crainey; sub: Boyd); Larsson, Sutton.

went one way and then another before rolling a left-foot effort home to be greeted with the Parkhead followers' version of the Hampden Roar.

Martin O'Neill smiled: "I've almost run out of things to say about Henrik – he is a fantastic player. He would score goals in any league in the world and that last one would have graced any Cup Final on any stage. He's my kind of player, that's for sure. In fact, he would be the best manager in the world's type of player."

The final word must, of course, go to Henrik Larsson. "The fact we survived with ten men and got stronger shows how much character we have in this side. It was difficult, but we fought for each other and that's why we won 3-0. Martin O'Neill has made the whole team want the ball – no-one is afraid. That is what he has given us. Our self-confidence is back and you need that."

Henrik Larsson and Martin O'Neill, a marriage made in Paradise.

Gould; Mjallby, Vega, Valgaeren; Healy, Lambert, Lennon, Moravcik (sub: Smith), Petta (sub: Crainey; sub: Boyd); Larsson and Sutton. ◼

CHEERS...Stephen Crainey, Jonathan Gould, Joos Valgaeren, Colin Healy, Jamie Smith and Henrik Larsson after the League Cup victory.

It's Trebles All Round

CELTIC 3
HIBS 0
(May 26, 2001)

THE Hampden meeting between Martin O'Neill's Celtic and Alex McLeish's Hibs had been called "The Green Party".

Nice title, but totally inaccurate because neither team were allowed to wear their normal strips and both had to play in their change strips; the Parkhead men in their gold tops and the Easter Road side in white shirts.

O'Neill didn't concern himself with the SFA's newly-found fixation with colour clashes and, instead, sent out his strongest team as he attempted a clean sweep in his first season in Scotland. Henrik Larsson, hat-trick hero against Kilmarnock in the League Cup Final, was in his usual place alongside his trusted ally Chris Sutton.

Alas, little Slovakian maverick Lubomir Moravcik lasted a mere eighteen minutes before hobbling off to be replaced by

HOOPS! WE DID IT... Celtic players changed into their traditonal green and white shirts following the 3-0 Scottish Cup Final win over Hibs at Hampden to complete the fabulous silverware clean sweep.

BHOYS ZONE

MARTIN O'NEILL marked his Old Firm managerial debut with a 6-2 win over Rangers on August 27, 2000. It was the most goals Celtic had scored against the Ibrox side since the 7-1 League Cup Final in 1957/58.

Jackie McNamara. And it was the substitute who pushed the Hoops towards a half-time advantage when he was set up by Larsson who sent him free into the box with a neat pass.

McNamara took an awkward first touch, but recovered in an instant to spear a low shot wide of the motionless Nick Colgan. He drew praise from manager O'Neill afterwards who said: "Jackie took the first goal brilliantly and, naturally, I was very pleased with that. It was a great pass from Henrik, but he still had to put the ball in the net."

Three minutes after the break, Larsson whipped a first time effort from the edge of the box high into the net for the second goal and, with ten minutes to go, the unstoppable Swede was hauled to the ground by Gary Smith for referee Stuart Dougal to award a stick-on penalty-kick.

Larsson dispatched it with his usual excellence and as the ball thudded behind Colgan, the astonishingly prolific hitman realised he had notched up his fifty-third and final goal of an incredible season. Celtic had also claimed their thirty-first Scottish Cup.

Didier Agathe enjoyed scampering down the right in the wide, rolling spaces of the Hampden playing surface and teased and tormented Ulrik Laursen, the Easter Road left-back.

O'Neill, though, must have seen some qualities in the Danish defender because he invited him to join Celtic that summer. The thought of never having to again face Agathe in public under the gaze of thousands might have hastened his answer in the affirmative.

At the end, Larsson said: "We won the league early, then the League Cup and everyone had been going on about the treble and how much it would mean to the club. Now we can talk about it. Now there are no problems. This was the one I hadn't won yet in Scotland.

"However, I've won it today and I'm very, very pleased. The second goal gave us a bit more breathing space and then we could sit back a little bit and try to pick them off. When we got the penalty-kick that was it finished."

A smiling O'Neill added: "It's been an enormous season for everyone and to finish it off today in front of our supporters at a packed Hampden is just sensational. Today is about the players and the supporters. I'm so, so pleased for both sets. The players have had to rouse themselves again for another big occasion, but I never thought there would be a problem because there is no sign of tiredness.

Scottish Cup

January 28, 2001: First Round:
STRANRAER 1 Harty
CELTIC 4 Valgaeren, McNamara, Knox (og), Moravcik

Douglas; Boyd, Vega, Valgaeren (sub: Mjallby); Agathe, McNamara, Lennon, Thompson, Petta (sub: Lambert); Larsson (sub: Moravcik), Sutton.

February 17:   Second Round:
DUNFERMLINE 2 Skerla, Nicholson
CELTIC 2 Larsson (2)

Douglas; Boyd, Vega, Valgaeren (sub: Tebily); Agathe, Lambert, Lennon, Thompson, Petta (sub: Petrov); Larsson, Sutton.

March 7:   Replay:
CELTIC 4 Vega (2), Larsson (2,1 pen)
DUNFERMLINE 1 Thomson

Douglas; Mjallby, Vega, Valgaeren; Agathe, McNamara (sub: Petrov), Lennon, Moravcik, Thompson; Larsson (sub: Crainey), Johnson (sub: Lambert).

March 11:   Quarter-Final:
CELTIC 1 Larsson
HEARTS 0

Douglas; Mjallby (sub: Boyd), Vega, Valgaeren; Agathe, Petrov, Lambert, Lennon, Thompson; Larsson, Moravcik (sub: Johnson).

April 15:   Semi-Final:
CELTIC 3 Larsson (2,1 pen), McNamara
DUNDEE UNITED 1 Lilley

Douglas; Mjallby (sub: Boyd), Vega, Valgaeren; Agathe, Lambert, Lennon, Moravcik (sub: McNamara), Thompson; Larsson, Sutton.

May 26:   Final:
CELTIC 3 McNamara, Larsson (2,1 pen)
HIBS 0

Douglas; Mjallby, Vega, Valgaeren; Agathe, Lambert (sub: Boyd), Lennon, Moravcik (sub: McNamara), Thompson (sub: Johnson); Larsson, Sutton.

"As I said, Jackie took his goal magnificently and the second from Henrik so soon after half-time settled everything. Now I just want time to enjoy this before I even think about next season."

Neil Lennon added: "It's been unbelievable since I came up here in December. Honestly, I did not expect this to happen. Not at all. I thought I was coming up to join a team to give Rangers a run for their money in the league. We've surpassed everything that has been asked of us. I'm now going to take it easy for a few weeks and reflect on this season.

"Mind you, we have now set ourselves exceptional standards and we'll just have to do it all again next season."

Douglas; Mjallby, Vega, Valgaeren; Agathe, Lambert (sub: Boyd), Lennon, Moravcik (sub: McNamara), Thompson (sub: Johnson); Larsson and Sutton. ▪

Brendan Rodgers *profile*

> *For me, Celtic is the greatest club in the world. I have the privilege to manage it and while I manage it I want to make it the best I possibly can.*

IT **is inconceivable to imagine any of Celtic's previous seventeen managers enduring a more excruciating competitive debut than Brendan Rodgers.**

LINCOLN RED IMPS 1 CELTIC 0. That was the preposterous, nonsensical scoreline that ricocheted around European football on the Tuesday evening of July 12, 2016. It was a result so implausible it was met everywhere with outright incredulity.

Semi-professional teams from Gibraltar should not beat the champions of Scotland. The local cop should not score the winning goal.

Off the top of my head, I can only think of The Titanic having a more disastrous first appearance.

It was not the voyage of discovery the new Parkhead boss would have envisaged or anticipated when he agreed to take over from Ronny Deila exactly fifty-two days beforehand.

The Norwegian's two-year reign came to an end, mainly due to two unarguable factors: the abject failure of his team to respond to the challenge from a Rangers side – one not competent enough to claim Premiership status – during a dismal Scottish Cup semi-final performance that ended in the ignominy of a penalty-kick shoot-out exit. And his indisputable inability to make an impression among Europe's elite.

In the previous two campaigns, Deila, in my opinion, demonstrated he did not have the quality or the nous to deal with the game at that level. In his first season, Celtic failed to reach the Champions League group stages when they lost 1-0 at home to the mediocre Slovenians of NK Maribor, toppling out on a 2-1 aggregate. And that followed a remarkable reprieve when it was discovered Poland's Legia Warsaw had fielded an ineligible player – for only a couple of minutes – after they had coasted to a 6-1 aggregate triumph, winning home and away.

The following year, it was the turn of Malmo to end

▶

Scottish Premier League Table

P	Team	Pld	W	D	L	GF	GA	GD	Pts
1	Celtic	38	34	4	0	106	25	+81	106
2	Aberdeen	38	24	4	10	74	35	+39	76
3	Rangers	38	19	10	9	56	44	+12	67
4	St Johnstone	38	17	7	14	50	46	+4	58
5	Heart of Midlothian	38	12	10	16	55	52	+3	46
6	Partick Thistle	38	10	12	16	38	54	−16	42
7	Ross County	38	11	13	14	48	58	−10	46
8	Kilmarnock	38	9	14	15	36	56	−20	41
9	Motherwell	38	10	8	20	46	69	−23	38
10	Dundee	38	10	7	21	38	62	−24	37
11	Hamilton Academical	38	7	14	17	37	56	−19	35
12	Inverness Caledonian Thistle	38	7	13	18	44	71	−27	34

League Cup Final

November 27, 2017:
CELTIC 3 Rogic, Forrest, Dembele (pen)
ABERDEEN 0

Gordon; Lustig, Simunovic, Sviatchneko, Izaguirre; Brown, Rogic (sub: McGregor); Roberts (sub: Bitton), Armstrong, Forrest (sub: Griffiths); Dembele.

Scottish Cup Final

May 27, 2017: **CELTIC 2** Armstrong, Rogic
ABERDEEN 1 Hayes

Gordon; Lustig, Simunovic, Boyata, Tierney (sub: Rogic); Brown, Armstrong; Roberts (sub: Sviatchenko), McGregor, Sinclair; Griffiths.

HOME IS WHERE THE HEART IS...boyhood Celtic fan Brendan Rodgers lands his dream job with 13,000 fans turning out to welcome the new manager at Parkhead in May.

JOLLY RODGERS...Celtic boss Brendan looks delighted to be in charge of the Scottish champions. That's a winning manager with a winning style.

Celtic's hopes following a tepid display in the second leg in Sweden. Celtic arrived with a 3-2 advantage and that was dismantled after two routine corner-kicks had created panic in the penalty box, the second decisive goal, somehow so typical of the lacklustre showing, bouncing into the net off Hoops defender Dedryck Boyata.

So, around thirteen thousand joyous supporters, with expectation levels soaring to new highs, went along to Celtic Park on the pivotal afternoon of May 20 to welcome the new manager, a professional who, unlike the rookie Deila, had proved himself at the top table.

In season 2013/14, the Irishman had come so close to guiding Liverpool to their first English title since 1990. In their wisdom, though, the club's American owners decided to relieve their manager of his duties in October 2015, shortly after he had agreed a four-year extension.

A good friend of mine, a former top-class footballer, has always insisted the men who run football clubs wouldn't know the difference between a ball and a banana. Who am I to disagree?

Hasty decisions in this game have a habit of having the same effect as a boomerang. Derby County once dispensed with the services of a bloke called Brian Clough in 1973. Six years later, he won the first of back-to-back European Cups with Nottingham Forest. St Mirren's esteemed chairman Willie Todd sacked a young progressive manager in 1978. The team boss who was handed his P45 was Sir Alex Ferguson, who was just a plain mister back then. Coincidentally, he didn't do too badly in Europe with Aberdeen and Manchester United.

Brendan Rodgers wasn't on soccer's version of the scrapheap for too long. Parkhead chief executive Peter Lawwell interviewed the self-confessed Celtic supporter from the seaside village of Carnlough, County Antrim in Northern Ireland, for the vacant managerial post at the champions.

He arrived in the east end of Glasgow amid a fanfare from expectant fans. Rodgers won them over immediately. "I have been brought up with Celtic all my life, with my brothers, uncles and cousins all big supporters who still come to the games to this day, so I am fairly steeped in the tradition of Celtic and I'm obviously proud to be named as manager here."

As far as the green and white-bedecked followers were concerned, the words could have been set to music.

"I remember my first Celtic game," he continued. "It was 1984 and I was eleven years old when Celtic played Finn Harps in a friendly in Ireland. I will never forget that.

"When I was younger, because of safety concerns, my parents were reluctant to let me go over so much and it was only later on that I would come over and go to games. Whenever my father could take me, then he would do, but that was the first time I saw Celtic play live and it was a really special moment.

"It has been surreal, really. For a team I have supported all my life, to now be the manager is a humbling experience. I am privileged to be here.

"My family have taken it very emotionally. I have had brothers and uncles crying. For some of them, it was something they maybe hoped they would see in their lifetime. They weren't sure if it would happen because predominately I have been based down in England and working in football there, but, for me, it was about coming

SHOWING HIS TRUE COLOURS... Brendan Rodgers waves his Celtic scarf at his new fans. The Premiership trophy, won the previous season, is displayed behind him. He would get his hands on it a year later!

to a massive club and there are not too many bigger than Celtic.

"I have a great background knowledge of this club and it makes me very determined to do well here as I am following a historic line of managers including Jock Stein, Billy McNeill, Davie Hay and Tommy Burns, some outstanding Celtic legends, so I'm very honoured to be here and following in their footsteps.

"I am only the eighteenth manager in the history of the football club and you go through that list of names I grew up with all my life and to be able to take over and continue that work of the Celtic manager with the back drop of those legends is very humbling and very emotional, but also a great privilege."

Rodgers realised only too well the awesome responsibility that had been placed upon his forty-four-year-old shoulders. He added: "For me, the objectives are pretty clear; to continue with the domination of Scottish football and also to make an impact in European football as this club is steeped in that tradition. You obviously go back to 1967 when Celtic became the first club from these islands to win the European Cup. There is a huge history here for the club in Europe."

So far, so good for the Irishman. Until the forty-eighth minute of his initial competitive confrontation, the first leg of the Champions League second round qualifier. The tie was viewed as a potential banana skin. The shabby, unkempt artificial playing surface would prove to be a great leveller in terms of minimising the quality of the visiting players. The conditions were never going to favour Celtic. And so it proved.

In front of a meagre crowd of 1,632, the second-half was only three minutes old when Efe Ambrose misjudged a long ball down the middle into Celtic territory. It looked like a routine clearance. However, Lee Cascario, a thirty-four-year-old Ministry of Defence police officer, took advantage of the Nigerian defender's fatal error and slid the ball beyond the exposed Craig Gordon. Leigh Griffiths twice struck the woodwork, but the face-saving equaliser wasn't in this particular script.

Red Imps captain Roy Chipolina, a thirtysomething local Customs Officer, was in no mood to play down the achievement of the minnows. He declared delightedly: "This is the biggest shock in European footballing history." It was difficult to mount a cogent argument.

However, the latest incumbent of the Celtic dug-out, at least proved he did not possess a panic button. While the world apparently collapsed around his ears, he said: "There's no embarrassment," adding: "It was a tough game in tough conditions.

"We dominated and had enough chances, but sometimes it can happen like that – one ball up the pitch and they're in. They took their chance. You let the local team have their night, we press on, another week's training and be better for it. It's a two-legged affair and our objective is to get through. The message for our fans is to stay calm."

A week later, 55,632 followers turned out on a balmy Glasgow evening to witness Celtic winning the second leg 3-0 with three quickfire goals in seven first-half minutes from Mikael Lustig, Leigh Griffiths and Patrick Roberts. The Champions League adventure was still on; commendably, the manager had never been in any doubt.

With a calm assurance, Rodgers surveyed and sifted ▶

through his squad as the weeks ticked by. The unfortunate Efe Ambrose, a beacon for connoisseurs of calamity, would play one more game before being effectively shown the door. Others, such as Nadir Ciftci, Scott Allan, Saidy Janko, Kristoffer Ajer, Ryan Christie – all brought to the club by Ronny Deila – would find themselves playing football elsewhere on a loan basis. Little time was wasted on Norwegian midfielder Stefan Johansen, who was sold to Fulham following one fleeting appearance as a substitute.

WAVE OF JOY...Celtic boss Brendan Rodgers has that winning feeling – again!

Moussa Dembele, a raw nineteen-year-old French striker, made the journey in reverse to become Rodgers' first signing for Celtic, a mere £500,000 in a Development Fee changing hands for his services. The Irishman went into overdrive as he stamped his brand on his side. Scott Sinclair, a lavishly-skilled attacker he had worked with at Chelsea and Swansea City, arrived from Aston Villa in a deal that would rise to £4.5 million,

Dutch goalkeeper Dorus de Vries, another with whom Rodgers had a past association during their days at the Welsh outfit, cost £400,000 from Nottingham Forest and raiding right-back Cristian Gamboa, a Porta Rican international, was signed at the cost of £1 million from West Brom. Kolo Toure, the classy Ivorian central defender, who had a connection with the Celtic boss during their days at Liverpool, joined on a one-year deal as a free agent following his release by the Anfield outfit.

Rodgers further augmented his squad during the January transfer window when he brought in another Ivory Coast international, Eboue Kouassi, a nineteen-year-old midfield enforcer from Russian side Krasnodar at the cost of £2.8 million. The jigsaw puzzle was coming together.

An instant reward was the delivery of the League Cup trophy, won with a flourish and considerable style against Aberdeen at Hampden on the afternoon of November 27, 2016 with goals from Tom Rogic, James Forrest and Moussa Dembele, from the penalty spot. Celtic had gone through the competition without Craig Gordon being required to retrieve the ball from his net.

After guiding the team to their sixth successive Premiership crown with a five-goal annihilation of Hearts in Edinburgh on April 2, 2017, with eight games still to play, there was further good news for the jubilant Celtic supporters when Rodgers announced he would be signing a four-year extension to his contract.

Once again, the soothing articulation from the popular Irishman was nothing short of melodious to the ears of those of a Celtic persuasion.

"We always want to win the league and as long as I am here that will be the aim."

Was there some blarney involved when Rodgers insisted the deal had not been put in place for him still being around to help the club to the magical ten successive titles?

He answered: "The length of contract wasn't necessarily built around that. It was more of a commitment looking forward in terms of improvement, seeing some of our young players through from the academy.

"And it was going to be very hard for me to sit with Craig Gordon, Kieran Tierney, Tom Rogic and James Forrest and all these boys and ask them to commit their futures to Celtic while I was on a one-year rolling contract.

"It is a young squad, we have got some real good experience in there, as well, and over the course of four years that allows that group to develop and improve and I want to be a part of it.

"Players will always look at the manager and see how long he is connected to the club.

"If I am committed to the club fully, hopefully that makes it a little bit easier for them to make that decision. That is important and it felt right. I couldn't be happier. Personally, I'm in a great place.

"It's the beginning of the journey, we have only been here a short time. But there is a lot more to achieve in the development of the club and that is exciting.

"For me, Celtic is the greatest club in the world. I have the privilege to manage it and while I manage it I want to make it the best I possibly can.

"I just love being here, love helping the players develop and making the team better."

And, as Brendan Rodgers spoke, memories of a confounding July evening in Gibraltar drifted seemingly into the mists of a bygone era. ∎

JOY BHOYS...skipper Scott Brown and manager Brendan Rodgers with the Premiership trophy.

Rodgers' Rhapsody in Green

BRENDAN RODGERS was a mere three minutes from an impeccable record in his six encounters against Rangers in a truly memorable campaign as Celtic manager.

The man who wrecked the possibility of an Old Firm clean sweep was Ibrox veteran defender Clint Hill who scored a late goal in the 1-1 draw at Parkhead in March.

Rodgers, though, might not have complained too much. He kicked off the six-game crusade with a 5-1 win in September – and completed the journey with a 5-1 triumph in April.

CELTIC 5 RANGERS 1
(September 10, 2016)

MIGHTY Moussa Dembele went on the rampage as he made his first appearance in the Glasgow derby, a game which can overpower even veterans of the fixture. The twenty-year-old striker, a bargain £500,000 signing from Fulham in the summer, looked as though he had been born for this big-time stage.

The awesomely-built French ace was brought in to replace the injured Leigh Griffiths and simply ran amok with a phenomenal and perfect hat-trick – one with his head, one with his right foot and one with his left. It was a pulverising performance from Dembele who had the huge percentage of the 60,000 audience at a rocking Parkhead in raptures.

Remarkably, it took Celtic until the thirty-fourth minute to claim the breakthrough goal. Scott Sinclair swung over a

> **MOUSSA DEMBELE** was Brendan Rodgers' first signing for the club in the summer of 2016 at a cost of £500,000. By January the prolific French hitman was being valued at £30 million.

left-wing corner-kick and the juggernaut frontman was unmarked as he sent a header thudding into the net. Eight minutes later, Dembele doubled his team's advantage when he latched onto a threaded pass from Nir Bitton, sold a supreme dummy to Phillipe Senderos and tucked the ball away with the outside of his right foot.

Just before the interval, Dorus de Vries, the keeper bought from Nottingham Forest to team up again with his former Swansea manager Brendan Rodgers, elected to remain on his line as James Tavernier swung over a right-wing cross. Kenny Miller met it at the back post to loop a header over the Dutch goalie and Joe Garner bundled the ball over the line from practically under the crossbar. The narrowness of the half-time scoreline was met with a fair bit of incredulity.

However, Celtic stretched their advantage again in the sixty-first minute when Man of the Match Dembele released a pass to Sinclair who finished with a fair amount of aplomb. In the eighty-first minute Rangers' new signing Senderos, who just couldn't cope with the energetic Gallic giant, was sent off following a second yellow card for a senseless handball. The former Swiss international looked almost relieved to be exiting the painful proceedings. Two minutes later, Dembele completed his terrific threesome when Mikael Lustig sent over a neat cross from the right and the frontman killed it in one movement before lashing a left-foot drive into the corner of the net.

Stuart Armstrong, who had replaced Tom Rogic in the fifty-fourth minute, made the most of some slick lead-up play between Sinclair and Kieran Tierney to thump a low drive beyond the overworked and exhausted Wes

SMILES BETTER...the Celts celebrate at Ibrox (left to right) Scott Brown, Callum McGregor, Leigh Griffiths, Jozo Simunovic and Scott Sinclair.

Foderingham for the fifth and final goal as the champions finished with a flourish. It had been a day to remember for a young Frenchman and a forty-four-year-old Irishman.

Rodgers said: "That's why it it's one of the greatest, if not the greatest derby, in the world. It was an incredible atmosphere and, of course, our performance lifts the crowd. It was a brilliant display from ourselves and a great result. A lot of these boys have travelled over 60,000 miles across the international break, so to come back and play at that intensity, that level and be that clinical was a joy to see.

"It does make it sweet when you play that well and perform with that concentration, so it was a very good performance. Moussa Dembele is a top talent, too. He scored three wonderful and different types of goals. But, of course, today was about the team."

De Vries; Lustig, Toure, Sviatchenko, Tierney; Brown (sub: McGregor), Bitton; Forrest (sub: Roberts), Rogic (sub: Armstrong), Sinclair; Dembele.

WHACK...Scott Sinclair thumps a shot past sliding Rangers defender Clint Hill as team-mate Tom Rogic looks on. Rob Kiernan and Lee Hodson get an anxious close-up view.

FRENCH FANCY...Moussa Dembele leaves Rangers keeper Matt Gilks helpless with the winner in the League Cup semi-final. Rob Kiernan is too late to intervene.

CELTIC 1
RANGERS 0
(October 23, 2016)

BRENDAN RODGERS **guided his team to within ninety minutes of being crowned Celtic Centurians with a masterclass performance to claim a place in the League Cup Final. Moussa Demble, swiftly becoming the destroyer of dreams around Govan way, netted the only goal with a touch of French chic three minutes from time.**

The Parkhead side's overall superiority was not reflected in the final result as they claimed their rightful place at Hampden for a silverware showdown on November 27. Only Aberdeen now stood between Celtic and their 100th major trophy.

Rodgers and his players must have wondered if it was going to be one of those days when nothing goes your way. Four minutes after the interval, Erik Sviatchenko rose above Clint Hill to propel a header wide of keeper Matt Gilks' groping fingers. However, the cries of "Goal" were strangled among the Celtic contingent when referee Craig Thomson unfathomably ruled it out. The match official indicated a push by the Dane, but TV pictures clearly showed it was a fifty/fifty challenge without an infringement from the Celt.

In the sixty-seventh minute, Andy Halliday was punished for a reckless challenge on Scott Brown twenty-five yards out. Scott Sinclair elected to take the free-kick and curled it high above Gilks. Unfortunately, it struck the bar, touched the goalie's glove on the way out and, defying gravity, dropped behind the fallen No.1 who was able to grab the ball on the line.

However, as the semi-final edged towards extra-time and, even worse, dreaded penalty-kicks, Celtic finally got their reward. Jozo Simunovic, who was playing instead of Kolo Toure who had gifted Borussia Monchengladbach both their goals in their shock 2-0 win at Parkhead in midweek, was the architect with a long-range defence-splitting pass. Left-back Lee Wallace failed to cut out the ball and Leigh Griffiths, on for Tom Rogic, was onto it in a flash.

His cross was perfection and Dembele displayed the cheek of a confident performer at the height of his game as he cleverly backheeled the ball through the legs of the surprised Gilks and into the net. It was a worthy, if belated, winner. Now there was only the little matter of taking care of the Dons at the national stadium the following month.

Rodgers said: "I thought we were very dominant in terms of chances, power, quality and strength. How we went about the game was brilliant. The players stopped them building and the intensity of the press we were able to put on them was at a real high level. When we had the ball, we created opportunities and looked a real threat going forward.

"So, in every element of our game, it was at a high level. When you consider coming off the back of a really tough Champions League game in midweek, every single one of the players deserve a huge amount of credit for not only their performance, but their strength and mentality to get the victory."

Gordon; Lustig, Simunovic, Sviatchenko, Tierney; Brown, Bitton (sub: Armstrong); Forrest (sub: Gamboa), Rogic (sub: Griffiths), Sinclair; Dembele.

RANGERS 1
CELTIC 2
(December 31, 2016)

CELTIC had already played eight games in December as they prepared for the Hogmanay confrontation at Ibrox. With praiseworthy and phenomenal consistency, Brendan Rodgers' side had won seven of those outings with the other drawn, a 1-1 Champions League stalemate against Manchester City at The Etihad.

Motherwell, Partick Thistle (twice), Hamilton Accies (twice), Dundee and Ross County had been met and vanquished en route to the third meeting of the season against Mark Warburton's team in Govan before bringing down the curtain on an eventful 2016 for all concerned with the Parkhead club.

Celtic knew a win would see them go nineteen points ahead of their Glasgow neighbours, a victory that would most assuredly leave them in their slipstream for the rest of the league season. However, the task became a bit more onerous when Rangers took the lead in the twelfth minute.

eluded his marker Danny Wilson at the far post. He took a touch with his right foot and then lashed in an unstoppable left-foot piledriver that exploded into the roof of the net.

Ten minutes after the turnaround, the French striking sensation almost repeated the feat when he met a deft left-wing cross from Callum McGregor in acrobatic fashion, but the ball bounced up off the turf past a bamboozled Foderingham and clattered against the face of the crossbar and the chance was lost.

Celtic were not to be denied, though. In the sixty-eighth minute, Rodgers took off James Forrest and introduced substitute Patrick Roberts. It turned out to be a shrewd move from the manager. Within two minutes, the tricky, little winger helped set up the winner. He dinked a lovely pass through the home rearguard into the path of the storming Armstrong on the right. He wasted no time in squaring it across the face of the goal and Sinclair had read his intentions perfectly. He was left in splendid isolation to roll the ball into the net at the back post.

Rodgers said: "I thought it was a brilliant result and a really great advert for Scottish football. Both sets of players did very, very well considering the conditions. But I thought we thoroughly deserved to win it. In the first-half, we didn't start so well and didn't pass the ball so well, but we were always a threat on the counter-attack, trying to exploit the space.

HAPPY HOGMANAY...Scott Sinclair notches the winner with a close-range shot beyond Rangers keeper Wes Foderingham. Rob Kiernan gets that sinking feeling in the Hoops 2-1 triumph at Ibrox.

Danish defender Erik Sviatchenko played a role with an untypical sloppy pass straight to Kenny Miller. He knocked it wide to James Tavernier, who played a quick one-two with Josh Windass to get round the back of the defence before zipping a right-wing cross into the penalty area. Miller, racing in at speed, turned the ball home from three yards.

In the thirty-third minute, groans were exchanged for grins among the travelling support when Rodgers' side equalised. Moments earlier, Scott Sinclair had left Wes Foderingham helpless with a sweeping low effort that smacked against the inside of the left-hand upright before Clint Hill hastily booted the rebound for a corner-kick. Sinclair stepped up to take the award and Moussa Dembele, scorer of four goals in the two previous Old Firm meetings,

"We needed to readjust one or two things at half-time and I thought, in the second-half, we were brilliant. We looked a real threat and every time we went forward we looked like scoring. I'm disappointed just to get two goals. But the most pleasing thing of all is how we dealt with the pressure of falling behind in the game.

"We had talked about that before the match. How to find solutions and how to stay calm. Once we got the goal, we played our way back into the game again, so it was an outstanding performance, particularly in the second-half."

Gordon; Lustig, Simunovic, Sviatchenko, Izaguirre; Brown, Armstrong; Forrest (sub: Roberts), McGregor, Sinclair; Dembele.

▶

CELTIC 1
RANGERS 1
(March 12, 2017)

THE clock was ticking down as Celtic protected Stuart Armstrong's thirty-fifth minute effort. They looked comfortable enough, but calamity struck in the eighty-seventh minute when some unusually lackadaisical defending allowed an opening for the Ibrox men. Emerson Hyndman was presented with a clear shot at goal from just inside the box and the on-loan Bournemouth midfielder fired in a ferocious low drive.

Craig Gordon, as he had demonstrated throughout the game, was equal to the task. He spread his 6ft 4in frame as he somersaulted to his right to push the ball away. Alas, it went straight to veteran centre-half Clint Hill, lurking at the far post. Before Mikael Lustig could react, the defender, with reflexes belying his thirty-eight years, sped in to snap up the opportunity from practically on the goal-line to ram the equaliser into the net.

Apart from a pocket of visiting fans, Celtic Park fell silent; no-one saw that one coming. It looked as though another three points were about to be claimed after the first-half opener from Armstrong, who had earlier struck the post with a clever free-kick. Dame Fortune changed her snarl to a smile shortly afterwards when he worked a swift manoeuvre with James Forrest and smashed a sizzling left-foot drive from sixteen yards low past Wes Foderingham at his left-hand post.

The encounter ended on a controversial note when referee Bobby Madden refused what looked to many like an indisputable penalty-kick in the fading seconds. Hill, who had previously been booked, clearly attempted to pull back Leigh Griffiths outside the box before the elusive striker raced clear. The defender then lunged in to send the Celtic player crashing to the ground. Penalty-kick? It certainly would have been given by most match officials, but, astoundingly, Madden waved away the claims.

In the end, Celtic had to be content with a draw that kept them thirty-three points ahead of the Ibrox side. They also knew they would lift their sixth successive Premiership crown if they won their next two games against Dundee and Hearts.

Rodgers said: "We obviously should have had a penalty-kick right at the death. It was a clear-cut penalty. It's very frustrating, especially when Clint Hill tells me he got away with it on the pitch, so that's even more so. Clint's a good guy, an honest fella and I know when he says it, he knows he got away with one. Probably everyone has seen it apart from the referee.

"It's always disappointing if you lose an equaliser late on like that, especially the manner of it. But that's the way it

THE RACE IS ON...and the winner is Kieran Tierney as he gets away from Rangers' Lee Hodson.

goes sometimes. I'm proud of the team, although I don't think we were so good in the first-half. However, I thought the commitment was great and, in the second-half, I thought it was maybe a matter of time before we got our second goal, but when it's at 1-0 there is always that little moment that can happen."

Gordon; Lustig, Boyata, Sviatchenko, Tierney; Brown, Bitton (sub: McGregor); Forrest (sub: Roberts), Armstrong (sub: Griffiths), Sinclair; Dembele.

CELTIC 2
RANGERS 0
(April 23, 2017)

THE Celtic cavalcade rolled into Hampden and produced a command performance as they majestically booked a place in the Scottish Cup Final against Aberdeen on May 27. Brendan Rodgers' side were so much in control with their quality play the game could have been dubbed Bhoys v Boys. Rangers didn't stand a chance in the High Noon shoot-out.

The Parkhead side opened the scoring in the eleventh minute and the Ibrox side, with Portuguese coach Pedro Caixinha taking charge of them in an Old Firm game for the first time, were already heading for the tournament's exit. Their defence was prised open with consummate ease. Mikael Lustig launched a long ball from his own half towards the menacing Moussa Dembele. The French marksman's first touch was exquisite as he plucked it out of the air on the toe of his boot before knocking a pass inside to Callum McGregor. Combining confidence and composure, the midfielder, from twenty yards, simply passed the ball beyond the flummoxed and static Wes Foderingham at his right-hand side.

Celtic's possession play was awesome as they outplayed their opponents in the opening forty-five minutes and Rangers' only response – if you could call it that – was a wayward long-range effort from Kenny Miller that sailed harmlessly over the crossbar. It was all over as a contest three minutes after the turnaround. Dedryck Boyata broke up an attack just inside the Celtic box before passing accurately to Patrick Roberts on the right. With perfect precision, he placed the ball in front of the sprinting Leigh Griffiths, who had taken over from hamstring victim Dembele before half-time.

Last season's forty-goal man was crudely brought crashing to the ground by a last-ditch James Tavernier tackle. Referee Willie Collum pointed to the spot and all eyes were on Scott Sinclair, who had missed his previous attempt in the 1-1 draw against Partick Thistle only three games earlier. Foderingham made a gallant effort to thwart him, but the power of the flamboyant attacker's well-struck drive was enough to beat him at his right-hand post.

Gordon was awakened from his slumber to deal with a close-range header from Miller and then he blocked a shot from the same player with his foot, but there could be little doubt his team-mates had taken their foot off the gas with the result never in doubt. The Scotland international goalkeeper also looked lively to turn a soaring twenty-yard drive from Joe Dodoo round the left-hand upright. It was Celtic, though, who came closest to scoring again when substutute Tom Rogic, on for McGregor, torpedoed in a low shot from outside the box that had Foderingham beaten. However, the ball struck the base of the right-hand post and whipped harmlessly past.

Celtic and their manager were now set for the grand finale to an exceptional campaign.

Rodgers said: "In general, we were outstanding. We deservedly went one-nil up, had other opportunities and restricted Rangers to very few efforts. Young Callum McGregor was brilliant, really, really good, technically gifted and it was a wonderful goal he scored. Everyone's delighted, it's one of the best team performances we've had all season.

"Before the game, we said to ourselves if we set out the first ten minutes at one hundred per cent, keep the ball and create chances, there's no doubt we'll win the game. Now we can looking forward to the Cup Final. I'm sure if we can play as well as we did in the League Cup Final against them, or like we did on this occasion, it could be a great day for us, but there's a lot of hard work between now and then.

"We are one game away from a real historic season."

Gordon; Lustig, Simunovic, Boyata, Tierney; Brown, Armstrong; Roberts (sub: Forrest), McGregor (sub: Rogic), Sinclair; Dembele (sub: Griffiths). ▶

MIGHTY MOUSSA...unstoppable French hitman Dembele celebrates one of his five goals against Rangers during his memorable first season at the champions.

CHEERS AND TEARS...Jozo Simunovic leads the celebrations as Stuart Armstrong races to congratulate scorer Moussa Dembele after his equaliser in the 2-1 Hogmanay win at Ibrox.

RANGERS 1
CELTIC 5
(April 29, 2017)

CELTIC won their 100th trophy when they beat Aberdeen 3-0 in the League Cup Final at Hampden on November 27. Tom Rogic, James Forrest and Moussa Dembele (pen) scored the goals.

RANGERS were swept away by a green-and-white whirlwind as Celtic hammered in five goals at Ibrox for the first time in their history. Brendan Rodgers' team started at a furious tempo and maintained the onslaught throughout in an incredibly one-sided encounter.

The visitors took the lead in the seventh minute and were relentless as they hunted down their foes in pursuit of even more glory. A last-ditch tackle from Clint Hill prevented Callum McGregor from opening the scoring in sixty-five seconds, but he only delayed the inevitable agony. Teenage left-back Myles Beerman was reckless with a sliding challenge on speeding Patrick Roberts and he sent the winger sprawling in the penalty box. Referee John Beaton pointed to the spot and Scott Sinclair, as he had done the previous week, sent the ball spinning into the corner of the net, this time with Wes Foderingham guessing wrong and going the wrong way.

In the eighteenth minute, the crestfallen keeper revisited the back of his rigging to fetch the ball for a second time. Stuart Armstrong showed more desire in a challenge for the ball with Emerson Hyndman and took possession before releasing a pass to Leigh Griffiths on the left. He took a touch

and, from an angle, unleashed a mighty left-foot drive that zoomed over the goalie's hands into the net. The procession towards the Rangers goal continued unabated for the remaining twenty-seven minutes of the half. Griffiths battered one off the crossbar and, astoundingly, Sinclair put the rebound wide of the gaping target. The Englishman, voted the Celtic Player of the Year by his team-mates, then missed from two yards after a dainty lob over from the left by Griffiths.

The second-half was only seven minutes old when the champions struck again. The debonair Roberts retrieved a misplaced pass to poke the ball in front of McGregor, who resisted the temptation to hit a first-time shot. He nurtured the ball, waited for a moment and then placed a cunning shot through the legs of James Tavernier and wide of the sprawling Foderingham. In the sixty-sixth minute, the flustered Beerman clattered Roberts once again and Griffiths delicately swung over the resultant free-kick. The keeper was rooted to his line and Dedryck Boyata took full advantage as he rose to nod the ball down and into the net.

There was a moment's respite for the well-trounced home side in the eighty-first minute when Kenny Miller worked a quick one-two with Joe Garner and placed a neat effort wide of the exposed Craig Gordon. Celtic kept the best to the last. Three minutes remained when Mikael Lustig picked up a loose ball and careered towards the danger zone. Displaying the skills of a Messi or a Ronaldo, the Swedish international defender danced his way past Danny Wilson, lined up a shot from the edge of the box and gracefully caressed the ball towards its destination.

Rodgers said: "It was an outstanding team performance. From the very first whistle, we were exceptional. The only disappointment was we could have scored more goals. We created really good chances to get more. Fundamentally, the players pressed the game very well. Our tactical organisation for getting the ball back was the key.

"A lot of our game has improved as the season has gone on. I said when I came in, we would get better and better. If you compare this 5-1 to the 5-1 earlier this season, there's a big difference for me in terms of tactical organisation and players understanding concepts of what we are trying to do. Collectively, they all understand their roles in getting forward, who needs to score goals and who needs to be effective."

Gordon; Lustig, Simunovic, Boyata, Tierney; Brown (sub: Kouassi), Armstrong (sub: Rogic); Roberts (sub: Forrest), McGregor, Sinclair; Griffiths. ∎

BLACK, GOLD AND GLORY...Leigh Griffiths and James Forrest celebrate a goal against St Johnstone in Perth with unconfined joy.

Six of the Best

WELCOME TO THE CLUB...Celtic fans get their first sight of Scott Sinclair as he warms up before coming on as a substitute for his dream debut against Hearts, netting the winning goal.

HEARTS 1
CELTIC 2
(August 7, 2016)

THE Celtic support swiftly understood why Brendan Rodgers had been so determined in his quest to sign his former Swansea City player Scott Sinclair. One look at the flamboyant attacker was all it took.

The Parkhead manager had tracked the left-sided raider for about a month before he finally got his man with Aston Villa accepting a fee that would rise to £4.5million with add-ons. Money well spent, declared the champions' followers in the near-17,000 Tynecastle crowd after witnessing Sinclair in action for under half-an-hour.

The Englishman only agreed the deal the previous afternoon and Celtic rushed through his registration to make sure he was eligible to play against the Edinburgh side. Rodgers left him on the subs' bench at the start, but he replaced Stuart Armstrong in the sixty-first minute with the score stalemated at 1-1.

Rodgers applauded his side's first goal in the Premiership in the eighth minute when Callum McGregor was sent spinning under a challenge and the ball broke to James Forrest. Without breaking stride, the winger struck the ball with the outside of his right foot from the edge of the box and his screamer left Jack Hamilton helpless low to his right.

Referee John Beaton mistakenly awarded the Edinburgh side a penalty-kick in the thirty-sixth minute after Jamie Walker had taken an obvious dive when Kieran Tierney checked out of a tackle. The whistler was conned and Walker was later banned for simulation. That was of little consequence to Celtic, however, when Walker drilled the award beyond Craig Gordon.

The game looked to be heading for a draw until the entrance from Sinclair and his immediate impact. Running more than half the length of the field as Rodgers' men hit on the break, the new Bhoy arrived smack on time to hammer a sublime left-wing delivery from Leigh Griffiths into the net for the winner.

Justice was done. During a rollicking, entertaining clash, eleven players were booked – four from Celtic – and Sinclair is hardly likely to forget his introduction to Scottish football.

Gordon; Lustig, Toure, O'Connell (sub: Rogic), Tierney; Brown, Armstrong (sub: Sinclair); Forrest, McGregor, Griffiths (sub: Janko); Dembele.

CELTIC 4
ABERDEEN 1
(August 27, 2016)

ABERDEEN arrived at Parkhead hoping to stop the rot. The Pittodrie outfit had lost on their previous TWENTY-TWO visits to the east end of Glasgow in twelve years of misery while also conceding a landslide sixty-two goals.

Before the twelfth minute, they knew they could be in trouble again. Tom Rogic clattered one off the crossbar from twenty yards early in the encounter, but the Dons' good fortune only lasted a few more minutes. James Forrest prodded the ball in front of Leigh Griffiths, who cheekily nutmegged Kenny McLean before thumping an unstoppable eighteen-yard left-foot drive in-off the left-hand post.

All roads led to Joe Lewis in the visitors' goal, but, remarkably, the Pittodrie side drew level in the thirty-second minute when Adam Rooney latched onto a Kolo Toure mis-hit clearance and curled a right-foot effort past new keeper Dorus de Vries. However, James Forrest restored the lead three minutes from the interval when he beautifully swerved the ball past Lewis from fourteen yards following a peach of a pass from Rogic.

The one-way procession continued in the second period, but Celtic had to wait until three minutes from the end to add to their tally. Mark Reynolds, who had earlier been booked for a cynical trip on Rogic, bundled over Scott Sinclair in the box and saw yellow again before making his exit. Sinclair drilled the award low to the keeper's right as Lewis took off for his left.

Dons' away day agonies were complete when Rogic swept in a devastating free-kick for the goal his all-round play deserved.

De Vries; Lustig, Toure, Sviatchenko, Tierney; Brown, Bitton (sub: McGregor); Forrest, Rogic, Sinclair; Griffiths (sub: Dembele). ▶

WIZARD OF OZ...Tom Rogic in a tussle with Aberdeen captain Ryan Jack.

BHOYS

CELTIC dropped their first league points of the season when a stoppage-time goal from Alex Fisher gave Inverness Caley Thistle a 2-2 draw in the Highlands on September 18. The champions won their next twenty-two Premiership games before a Clint Hill goal three minutes from time gave Rangers a 1-1 draw at Parkhead on March 12.

ZONE

ABERDEEN 0
CELTIC 1
(October 29, 2016)

BRENDAN RODGERS realised this confrontation would be something of a litmus test in the early days of his Celtic managerial career. The Parkhead men, under Ronny Deila's leadership, had lost twice – both 2-1 – at Pittodrie the previous season.

Those defeats represented half of the total losses in the Premiership – Motherwell and St Johnstone also overcame the champions – and the Dons had completed the campaign as runners-up to Deila's outfit for the second successive year, fifteen points adrift.

So, Rodgers would have taken his side to the Granite City on a breezy afternoon with the thought they could be his team's main challenger in his debut season at his boyhood favourites. In short, Derek McInnes' men had to be put in their place with a new Bhoy in town.

As expected, it was an extremely competitive affair and it took a gem of a goal and an extraordinary save to separate two able combatants at the end of a nerve-shredding ninety minutes.

The matchwinner arrived in the twenty-third minute and it was claimed by Antipodean artiste Tom Rogic, who was clearly revelling in the coaching of Rodgers to become a key player within the structure of the Irishman's team.

Dons right-back Shay Logan was wayward with a headed clearance and the alert midfielder was on to it in a flash. He took a touch before elegantly placing an effort off the outside of his left foot wide of Joe Lewis from twenty yards. It was a sublime strike.

It remained that way until the dying seconds when the home side were awarded a free-kick in a dangerous area. James Maddison, a talented young midfielder on loan from Norwich City, flighted the ball to practically under Craig Gordon's crossbar. There was the usual scrum and burly Adam Rooney threw himself into the mix.

It looked as though he had barged Erik Sviatchenko in the back and the Dane inadvertently got his head to the ball about two yards out to send it hurtling towards the top corner of the net. With blinding reflexes, Gordon reacted in an instant to throw up a hand and send the zooming object spiralling over his crossbar.

The combination of a goal and a save, both in the wonder category, proved irresistible on the day and Rodgers took his bow at Pittodrie in splendid style.

Gordon; Lustig (sub: Gamboa), Simunovic, Sviatchenko, Izaguirre; Brown, Rogic (sub: Bitton); Forrest (sub: Roberts), Armstrong, Sinclair; Dembele.

CELEBRATIONS AND CONGRATULATIONS…title-winners Tom Rogic, Gary Mackay-Steven, James Forrest, Kieran Tierney, Liam Henderson, Scott Brown and Craig Gordon.

MOTHERWELL 3
CELTIC 4
(December 3, 2016)

THEY'RE obviously not a superstitious lot over at Celtic Park. On the thirteenth Premiership outing of the season, they went in at half-time trailing by two goals to a lively Fir Park outfit. And yet no-one in the visitors' dressing room was willing to concede – or even contemplate – defeat.

Brendan Rodgers had to work quickly and thoughtfully in the intervening fifteen minutes to alter his team to combat the challenge of opponents who had managed to pierce their armoury twice in the opening forty-five minutes – which was something no-one had managed to achieve in ten hours of domestic football leading up to this game.

Craig Gordon and his rearguard had proved to be unbreakable, but they were undone in only three minutes at Fir Park with the simplest of goals. Former Celtic skipper Stephen McManus shelled the ball downfield from deep in his own half. Experienced Ivorian international defender Kolo Toure, who had rejoined his former Liverpool boss on a one-year deal in the summer, misjudged the flight of the ball.

Striker Louis Moult timed his run in behind the centre-half to absolute perfection and, with Gordon off his line, neatly cushioned an effort towards goal and the ball gently spun towards its destination. That wasn't in the script. In the thirty-fifth minute, Ross McLean raced free on the left wing before crossing to the backpost. Unfortunately, Toure's timing was off again and Moult materialsed in space again to knock the ball into the net. That DEFINITELY wasn't in the script.

Rodgers stressed the utter importance of an early goal in the second-half. Three minutes later, Callum McGregor, who had replaced Emilio Izaguirre, duly obliged after working a neat one-two with Stuart Armstrong. Celtic had to wait until the seventieth minute, though, before they drew level. Armstrong was again involved with an inviting left-wing cross and Patrick Roberts headed in from close range.

Unbelievably, Motherwell went ahead again inside sixty seconds. The Celtic defence was posted missing when Steven Hammell launched over a deep left-wing ball and Lionel Ainsworth was given the freedom of Lanarkshire as he came in from the right to lash an unstoppable effort wide of Gordon.

A crazy spell of three goals in as many minutes continued when, practically from the kick-off, Armstrong worked an

MR MAGIC...
Tom Rogic.

opening before turning and hitting a low shot away from the diving Craig Samson. Could Celtic conjure a winner?

With the referee looking at his watch, Tom Rogic meandered over to the left wing in search of the ball. He picked it up, a swift swivel of the hips threw a defender one way as he went another as he cut across the penalty box before arcing a delightful right-foot finishing effort low down at Samson's left-hand post.

It was a goal fit to win any game.

Rodgers admitted: "We were poor in the first-half. We got off to an awful start. We changed the system at half-time to 3-4-3. We were absolutely brilliant second-half. To score the four goals, to win the game, it really shows the mentality of the team.

"Across the team, I have to give them huge credit because we had to put risk in the game. They took on the risk and they got the reward. I'm delighted for them. That was a great victory for us and give credit to Motherwell, as well, because I thought that they were set up very, very well."

Motherwell boss Mark McGhee conceded: "We've played a really good Celtic team, they've fought back into it and eventually they've got a winning goal. We've just got to live with that, but our performance was good."

Gordon; Lustig, Simunovic, Toure, Izaguirre (sub: McGregor); Brown, Armstrong; Roberts (sub: Bitton), Rogic, Forrest (sub: Gamboa); Dembele. ▶

BY THE RIGHT... Scott Sinclair fires in a shot before St Johnstone defender Ricky Foster can intervene.

ST JOHNSTONE 2
CELTIC 5
(February 5, 2017)

CELTIC were toiling in Perth before Brendan Rodgers introduced Moussa Dembele to proceedings. A wonderful early strike from Liam Henderson had been nullified by Keith Watson's leveller and Craig Gordon was beaten again by a header from his own defender Dedryck Boyata.

However, the Parkhead boss unleashed his twenty-goal striker in the fifty-ninth minute. Just over half-an-hour later, the French Under-21 hitman had hoisted his season's total to twenty-three with a splendidly-taken hat-trick, his second of the campaign after his trio against Rangers in September.

The Perth outfit will complain long and loud about the penalty-kick award that allowed Dembele to level the scores with virtually his first touch of the ball. Referee Craig Thomson had no hesitation in pointing to the spot after a Kieran Tierney left-wing cross had hit the hand of Watson.

Possibly, on this occasion, fortune favoured Celtic, but Saints should have remembered they may have been more than a little lucky to still have eleven men on the field after Paul Paton had been merely yellow-carded for hacking down Nir Bitton from behind only minutes beforehand.

Dembele was composure itself as he placed the ball on the spot, took a short run-up and walloped a drive into the roof of the net as keeper Zander Clark took off for his right. With thirty minutes still to play, the champions went for the jugular, struck three more times and stretched their lead at the top of the Premiership to an extraordinary twenty-seven points.

Yet they had to fight for this victory after making life difficult for themselves, despite a whirlwind start that saw them a goal ahead in the sixth minute.

Gary Mackay-Steven missed an early opportunity when his finishing effort was weak and lacked direction. The ball was scrambled clear and Celtic kept it alive with Scott Brown sending birthday Bhoy Patrick Roberts, celebrating his twentieth birthday, in on goal again.

Once more, Clark managed to block the effort, but his luck ran out when the ball bounced to Henderson and he calmly took aim and slotted in an effort at the shotstopper's exposed right-hand post.

The Saints, however, equalised just after the half-hour mark. Danny Swanson drilled over a corner-kick and Watson leapt to bullet a header towards goal. It took a touch off skipper Brown as it raged into the far corner. Worse was to follow two minutes from the interval!

Swanson swung over a left-wing cross that was missed by David Wotherspoon at the near post. The unfortunate Boyata was in direct line behind him and the defender, who has scored two matchwinning goals against the Saints and Aberdeen in recent weeks, couldn't get out of the way. The ball struck him on the head and flew into the net beyond the flummoxed Gordon.

Boss Rodgers resisted the temptation to introduce top marksman Dembele at the start of the second-half, but the French ace did come on just before the hour for Mackay-Steven, who was having a frustrating afternoon against the hard-tackling Brian Easton.

Then came the leveller via the penalty spot and after the ball thumped into the rigging behind Clark, there was only going to be one winner. In the seventy-fifth minute, Mikael Lustig gathered a left-wing cross from Tierney before delivering a perfect pass in front of Dembele on the edge of the box.

He coolly sent a controlled right-foot effort low past the diving keeper to put the champions ahead. Six minutes afterwards, Roberts set up Scott Sinclair, who drove at the Perth rearguard throughout the encounter, and the Englishman slotted in his fourteenth league goal of the season.

Celtic were relentless as they piled forward in pursuit of a more handsome winning margin and it was no surprise when they claimed a fifth. And, equally, it was no surprise when it was Dembele who scored again after a neat bit of penalty-box trickery from Lustig and Callum McGregor to round off a fantastic team goal with every player getting a touch of the ball before it reached its destination. The twenty-year-old frontman almost casually swept the ball past Clark to bring down the curtain on an excellent personal performance.

Sportingly, gaffer Rodgers admitted his team got a rub

of the green with the penalty-kick award. The Irishman was sympathetic when asked if the decision was harsh. He answered honestly: "I think it is. It's one where if it's given against you, you're disappointed. I don't know what the boy can do there, obviously I'm happy we got it."

Gordon; Lustig, Boyata, Sviatchenko, Tierney; Brown, Bitton; Roberts (sub: Ciftci), Henderson (sub: McGregor), Mackay-Steven (sub: Dembele); Sinclair.

HEARTS 0
CELTIC 5
(April 2, 2017)

SCINTILLATING Scott Sinclair hit a scorching treble as he propelled Celtic to their sixth successive Premiership title.

What a difference a year has made in the career of the flamboyant English attacker – last season he was relegated from the Premier League with Aston Villa!

Sinclair was ustoppable as he tore the Hearts defence apart with his tantalising forays on the left flank. He collected the matchball after his terrific trio and he was helped in inflicting capital punishment in Edinburgh by goals from the dazzling Stuart Armstrong and the excellent Patrick Roberts.

Brendan Rodgers' men have gone unbeaten all season on the domestic front, dropping just four points to two late equalisers in thirty matches since the Northern Irishman's arrival. There was never a doubt Celtic were going to claim the crown as they swept their opponents aside with a devastating display of attacking football with the end product to match the lead-up player.

Sinclair's first goal in the twenty-fourth minute almost tore a hole in the net behind keeper Jack Hamilton. He worked a neat one-two with Roberts before racing through the static defence. The ball exploded from his right boot and hurtled high over the helpless Hamilton.

And that was the start of the green-and-white carnival.

There was more pain to come for the gallant custodian when Sinclair lashed another one past him for the second goal shortly afterwards. The Hoops were denied a third goal five minutes after the break when a harassed home defender turned the ball into his own net. Bizarrely, referee Kevin Clancy ruled it out for offside.

However, number three was only delayed a matter of moments as Kieran Tireney combined with Armstrong and the midfielder just can't do any wrong at the moment. He lashed it with his cultured right foot and the ball zipped past Hamilton.

In the sixty-second minute, the travelling fans were celebrating again when Callum McGregor set up Roberts and the on-loan winger showed he, too, could hit the ball with ferocious power. The goalie was beaten all ends up as it walloped into the back of his net.

Sinclair completed his first hat-trick for the Hoops from the penalty spot after he had been bowled over. Once again he allied power with precision as he sent his effort beyond the shell-shocked Hamilton.

Delighted Rodgers could afford to give defender Kolo Toure a rare outing late on, with the Ivorian not starting a game since December. The Celtic boss reckoned his team's hammering of Hearts was a fitting way for the club to clinch their sixth successive title.

He said: "It typified how they've been for the majority of the season – their attitude, determination, style and intensity. We knew it would be a tough game and to win a pressure game like that is a remarkable achievement from the players.

"We take the energy and hunger from training into games and, from a coaching perspective, that's great to see. The fans have been behind the team from day one. Everyone deserves a huge amount of credit – the players, staff and supporters."

Skipper Scott Brown said: "Football-wise, it's been top notch. The manager has recruited great players and brought belief to everyone. We have really pushed on this season."

Hat-trick hero Sinclair added: "It was a performance that was unbelievable from the whole team. We've still got work to do and the season is not over yet. We keep winning and that's the mentality here – to keep going.We take one game at a time. We've done so well, so we just have to keep going."

Gordon; Lustig (sub: Gamboa), Boyata (sub: Toure), Simunovic, Tierney; Brown, Armstrong; Roberts (sub: Mackay-Steven), McGregor, Forrest; Sinclair. ◾

BRENDAN RODGERS hailed his "infrangibles" after Celtic finished the Premiership campaign unbeaten over 38 games.

A run of 34 victories and four draws sealed a record 106-point tally as the club won their sixth title in a row.

The team were dubbed 'The Invincibles', but it wasn't a word the Irishman wanted to use.

He revealed he had a word with his players and said: "The word I said to them was infrangible. That was the word I wrote up on the paper.

"Stuart Armstrong understood it, but I did actually say: 'For those of you who don't understand I wrote the meaning below'. So 'to be unbroken', that is another word for their vocabulary.

"It hasn't really been a key feature up until probably Thursday night. Because there are so many things that are out of our control in this type of situation.

"But the players had arrived with a couple of games to go and then it's real, you can't hide from it. You have a chance to go through a whole season and not be beaten.

"But it's how we did it. The level of football, the tactical discipline and excitement they have given supporters has been incredible to watch.

"And they now stand alone in history.

"You only have to look at the past 100 years or so since it was done in the 1890s, to tell you the difficulty of achieving that.

"It's a monumental achievement by the players."

Premiership Results

August 7, 2016: **HEARTS 1** Walker (pen)
CELTIC 2 Forrest, Sinclair

Gordon; Lustig, Toure, O'Connell (sub: Rogic), Tierney; Forrest, Brown, Armstrong (sub: Sinclair), McGregor; Dembele, Griffiths (sub: Janko).

August 20: **ST JOHNSTONE 2** Swanson (pen), MacLean
CELTIC 4 Griffiths, Sinclair, Forrest, Christie

Gordon; Janko, Toure, O'Connell, Tierney; Brown, Bitton (sub: Henderson); Forrest (sub: Christie), Rogic, Sinclair; Griffiths (sub: Dembele).

August 27: **CELTIC 4** Griffiths, Forrest, Sinclair (pen), Rogic
ABERDEEN 1 Rooney

De Vries; Lustig, Toure, Sviatchenko, Tierney; Brown, Bitton (sub: McGregor); Forrest, Rogic, Sinclair; Griffiths (Dembele).

September 10: **CELTIC 5** Dembele (3), Sinclair, Armstrong
RANGERS 1 Garner

De Vries; Lustig, Toure, Sviatchenko, Tierney; Brown (sub: McGregor), Bitton; Forrest (sub: Roberts), Rogic (sub: Armstrong), Sinclair; Dembele.

September 18: **INVERNESS CALEY THISTLE 2** King, Fisher
CELTIC 2 Rogic, Sinclair

De Vries; Gamboa (sub: Simunovic), Lustig, Sviatchenko, Tierney; Brown, Rogic (sub: Armstrong); Roberts (sub: Forrest), McGregor, Sinclair; Dembele.

September 24: **CELTIC 6** Dembele (2), Forrest, Griffiths, Sinclair (pen), Rogic
KILMARNOCK 1 Coulibaly

De Vries (sub: Gordon); Lustig, Simunovic, Sviatchenko, Tierney; Brown, Bitton; Forrest, Rogic, Sinclair (sub: Roberts); Dembele (sub: Griffiths).

October 1: **DUNDEE 0**
CELTIC 1 Brown

Gordon; Lustig, Simunovic, Sviatchenko, Tierney; Brown, Bitton; Forrest (sub: Roberts), Rogic (sub: Griffiths), Sinclair (sub: Armstrong); Dembele.

October 15: **CELTIC 2** Sinclair, Dembele (pen)
MOTHERWELL 0

Gordon; Gamboa (sub: Griffiths), Simunovic, Sviatchenko, Tierney; Brown, Henderson; Forrest (sub: Toure), Armstrong (sub: Roberts), Sinclair; Dembele.

October 26: **ROSS COUNTY 0**
CELTIC 4 Roberts, Armstrong, Sinclair, Dembele

Gordon; Gamboa, Lustig, Sviatchenko, Izaguirre; McGregor, Henderson (sub: Sinclair); Roberts, Armstrong, Christie (sub: Dembele); Griffiths (sub: Bitton).

October 29: **ABERDEEN 0**
CELTIC 1 Rogic

Gordon; Lustig (sub: Gamboa), Simunovic, Sviatchenko, Izaguirre; Brown, Rogic (sub: Bitton); Forrest (sub: Roberts), Armstrong, Sinclair; Dembele.

November 5: **CELTIC 3** Sinclair, Griffiths, Rogic
INVERNESS CALEY THISTLE 0

Gordon; Lustig (sub: Izaguirre), Simunovic, Sviatchenko; Roberts, Brown (sub: Bitton), Armstrong, McGregor, Sinclair; Dembele (sub: Rogic), Griffiths.

November 18: **KILMARNOCK 0**
CELTIC 1 Armstrong

Gordon; Lustig, Boyata, Sviatchenko, McGregor; Brown, Armstrong; Roberts (sub: Rogic), Sinclair, Forrest (sub: Bitton); Dembele.

December 3: **MOTHERWELL 3** Moult (2), Ainsworth
CELTIC 4 McGregor, Roberts, Armstrong, Rogic

Gordon; Lustig, Simunovic, Tiure, Izaguirre (sub: McGregor); Brown, Armstrong; Roberts (sub: Bitton), Rogic, Forrest (sub: Gamboa); Dembele.

December 9: **PARTICK THISTLE 1** Lindsay
CELTIC 4 Armstrong (2), Griffiths, McGregor

Gordon; Gamboa, Lustig, Sviatchenko, Izaguirre; Brown, Armstrong; Roberts (sub: Dembele), Rogic (sub: McGregor), Mackay-Streven (sub: Christie); Griffiths.

December 13: **CELTIC 1** Griffiths
HAMILTON ACCIES 0

Gordon; Lustig, Simunovic, Sviatchenko; Brown, Armstrong; Roberts, Rogic, McGregor (sub: Mackay-Steven); Griffiths, Dembele (sub: Bitton).

December 17: **CELTIC 2** Griffiths, Bitton
DUNDEE 1 Haber

Gordon; Gamboa, Simunovic, Sviatchenko, Izaguirre; Bitton, Armstrong; Christie, Rogic (sub: McGregor), Mackay-Steven (sub: Sinclair); Griffiths (sub: Dembele).

December 20: **CELTIC 1** Sinclair
PARTICK THISTLE 0

Gordon; Gamboa, Lustig, Simunovic, Miller (sub: Izaguirre); Brown, Henderson; Roberts, McGregor, Sinclair (sub: Armstrong); Dembele (sub: Griffiths).

December 24: **HAMILTON ACCIES 0**
CELTIC 3 Griffiths, Armstrong, Dembele

Gordon; Gamboa, Lustig, Sviatchenko, Izaguirre; Brown, Armstrong; Roberts (sub: Bitton), McGregor, Sinclair (sub: Forrest); Griffiths (sub: Dembele).

December 28: **CELTIC 2** Sviatchenko, Armstrong
ROSS COUNTY 0

Gordon; Lustig, Simunovic, Sviatchenko, Izaguirre; Brown, Armstrong; Forrest (sub: Roberts), Christie (sub: Henderson), Sinclair; Griffiths (sub: Dembele).

December 31: **RANGERS 1** Miller
CELTIC 2 Dembele, Sinclair

Gordon; Lustig, Simunovic, Sviatchenko, Izaguirre; Brown, Armstrong; Forrest (sub: Roberts), McGregor, Sinclair; Dembele.

January 25, 2017:
CELTIC 1   Boyata
ST JOHNSTONE 0

Gordon; Gamboa (sub: Sviatchenko), Boyata, Simunovic, Tierney; Brown, Bitton; Forrest (sub: Roberts), Armstrong, Sinclair; Dembele (sub: Griffiths).

January 29:   **CELTIC 4**   McGregor, Sinclair (2, 1 pen), Roberts
HEARTS 0

Gordon; Gamboa (sub: Lustig), Boyata, Simunovic, Tierney; Brown, Bitton; Roberts (sub: Aitchison), McGregor, Forrest (sub: Henderson); Sinclair.

February 1:   **CELTIC 1**   Boyata
ABERDEEN 0

Gordon; Lustig, Boyata, Simunovic, Tierney; Brown, Bitton; Roberts (sub: Sviatchenko), McGregor (sub: Henderson), Forrest (sub: Mackay-Steven); Sinclair.

February 5:   **ST JOHNSTONE 2**   Watson, Boyata (og)
CELTIC 5   Henderson, Dembele (3, 1 pen), Sinclair

Gordon; Lustig, Boyata, Sviatchenko, Tierney; Brown, Bitton; Roberts (sub: Ciftci), Henderson (sub: McGregor), Mackay-Steven (sub: Dembele); Sinclair.

February 18:   **CELTIC 2**   Dembele (pen), Forrest
MOTHERWELL 0

Gordon; Lustig, Boyata, Simunovic, Tierney; Brown, Bitton (sub: McGregor); Forrest, Henderson (sub: Armstrong), Sinclair; Dembele.

February 25:   **CELTIC 2**   Dembele (2, 1 pen)
HAMILTON ACCIES 0

Gordon; Gamboa, Boyata, Sviatchenko, Tierney; Brown, Bitton; Forrest (sub: Mackay-Steven), Armstrong (sub: McGregor), Sinclair; Dembele (sub: Griffiths).

March 1:   **INVERNESS CALEY THISTLE 0**
CELTIC 4   Sinclair, Dembele (2), Armstrong

Gordon; Lustig, Boyata, Sviatchenko, Tierney; Brown (sub: Henderson), Bitton; Mackay-Steven (sub: McGregor), Armstrong, Sinclair; Dembele.

March 12:   **CELTIC 1**   Armstrong
RANGERS 1   Hill

Gordon; Lustig, Boyata, Simunovic, Tierney; Brown, Bitton (sub: McGregor); Forrest (sub: Roberts), Armstrong (sub: Griffiths), Sinclair; Dembele.

March 19:   **DUNDEE 1**   El Bakhtaoui
CELTIC 2   Simunovic, Armstrong

Gordon; Lustig, Boyata, Simunovic, Tierney; Brown, McGregor (sub: Kouassi); Forrest (sub: Roberts), Armstrong, Sinclair (sub: Sviatchenko); Dembele.

April 2:   **HEARTS 0**
CELTIC 5   Sinclair (3, 1 pen), Armstrong, Roberts

Gordon; Lustig (sub: Gamboa), Boyata (sub: Toure), Simunovic, Tierney; Brown, Armstrong; Forrest, McGregor, Sinclair; Roberts (sub: Mackay-Steven).

April 5:   **CELTIC 1**   Sinclair
PARTICK THISTLE 1   Azeez

Gordon; Lustig, Simunovic, Sviatchenko; Gamboa, Kouassi (sub: Armstrong), Bitton, Izaguirre (sub: Rogic); Roberts, McGregor (sub: Aitchison), Sinclair.

April 8:   **CELTIC 3**   Armstrong, Sinclair, Forrest
KILMARNOCK 1   Jones

Gordon; Lustig, Simunovic, Boyata, Tierney; Brown, Armstrong (sub: Kouassi); Forrest, McGregor (sub: Rogic), Sinclair; Roberts (sub: Dembele).

April 16:   **ROSS COUNTY 2**   Gardyne, Boyce (pen)
CELTIC 2   Tierney, Roberts

Gordon; Simunovic, Sviatchenko, Tierney; Brown, Armstrong; Forrest (sub: Roberts), McGregor, Rogic (sub: Gamboa), Sinclair; Dembele (sub: Griffiths).

April 29:   **RANGERS 1**   Miller
CELTIC 5   Sinclair (pen), Griffiths, McGregor, Boyata, Lustig

Gordon; Lustig, Simunovic, Boyata, Tierney; Brown (sub: Kouassi), Armstrong (sub: Rogic); Roberts (sub: Forrest), McGregor, Sinclair; Griffiths.

May 6:   **CELTIC 4**   Roberts (2), Boyata, McGregor
ST JOHNSTONE 1   MacLean

Gordon; Ralston, Simunovic, Boyata, Tierney; Bitton, Armstrong; Roberts (sub: Forrest), Rogic (sub: McGregor), Johnston (sub: Sinclair); Griffiths.

May 12:   **ABERDEEN 1**   Hayes
CELTIC 3   Boyata, Armstrong, Griffiths

Gordon; Lustig (sub: Sviatchenko), Simunovic, Boyata, Tierney; Rogic (sub: Bitton), Armstrong; Roberts, McGregor, Sinclair; Griffiths (sub: Forrest).

May 18:   **PARTICK THISTLE 0**
CELTIC 5   Griffiths (pen), Rogic, Roberts (2), McGregor

Gordon; Gamboa, Sviatchenko, Boyata (sub: Toure), Izaguirre; Brown, McGregor; Roberts, Rogic, Forrest (sub: Bitton); Griffiths (sub: Sinclair).

May 21:   **CELTIC 2**   Griffiths, Armstrong
HEARTS 0

Gordon; Gamboa (sub: Rogic), Simunovic (sub: Toure), Boyata, Tierney; Brown, Armstrong (sub: Sviatchenko); Roberts, McGregor, Sinclair; Griffiths.

HAPPY HAMPDEN BHOYS...skipper Scott Brown holds aloft the League Cup as his team-mates celebrate the 3-0 win over Aberdeen, the first trophy on the way to the treble.

Centurians!

CELTIC 3
ABERDEEN 0
(November 27, 2016)

THE moment Wizard of Oz Tom Rogic stepped inside Graeme Shinnie's challenge and switched the ball to his cultured left foot in the sixteenth minute, there was only going to one winner in the 2016/17 League Cup Final on a brisk, invigorating Sunday afternoon at Hampden.

Aberdeen had arrived at the national stadium on a tidal wave of positivity and promises and there were many who insisted the Pittodrie outfit had a genuine opportunity of postponing Celtic's bid for their 100th major piece of silverware. Those beliefs were buried amid the rubble of rash optimism before the interval had arrived.

Rogic, an Australian playmaker with the happy knack of conjuring magical goals out of nothing, had already put Derek McInnes' side twice to the sword during the season. He netted in the champions' 4-1 triumph in Glasgow in August and followed that up with the only goal of a tense Pittodrie occasion in October. Could he keep the run going in the Cup Final? Or had the Dons learned from their harsh lessons?

We didn't have long to wait for the answer. Jozo Simunovic determinedly pushed forward out of defence before sliding a pass in front of Rogic, idling on the right. With skipper Shimmie trying to force him down the line, the classy Celt cut inside onto his trusty left foot and curled a low shot past the stretching Joe Lewis. It was exquisite in its execution.

Twenty-four minutes after his team-mate's masterly strike, James Forrest latched onto a Rogic pass just inside his own half and jinked and shimmied his way through the heart of the retreating rearguard. Anthony O'Connor and James Maddison were beguiled by his neat and nimble footwork. The winger, rejuvenated under the guidance of Brendan Rodgers, drove with pace and menace as the fans in Mount Florida held their breath in expectation. The Celtic fraternity were not to be disappointed.

As a frantic Andy Considine attempted a last-ditch intervention, Forrest took aim and let fly from just inside the box and his deadly-accurate blast flew like an arrow straight and low past Lewis at his right-hand side. The ball strangled itself in the rigging behind the fallen Dons keeper at precisely the same moment the travelling supporters realised their dreams of a Hampden sensation had evaporated.

It was all over in the sixty-fourth minute when Forrest, producing a Man of the Match display, raced onto a pass from Rogic before being felled by O'Connor. Little doubt about the penalty-kick award and likewise the outcome as Moussa Dembele strode forward purposely and deftly piloted the ball into one corner as Lewis moved to the other.

On the rare occasions the Dons threatened, Craig Gordon was there to keep them at bay. The Scotland international, a month before his thirty-fourth birthday, had gone through the tournament without conceding a goal and he smiled afterwards: "That's always important for a goalkeeper and the men in front of him. And we've got guys who can score goals from all different angles going forward, so we're looking really good at the moment. It's a great team to be part of and we're in a good place going forward."

Emphasising the excellence of the Celtic showing was the fact they had played in a gruelling Champions League encounter against Lionel Messi-inspired Barcelona at Parkhead the previous Wednesday. They lost 2-0, but might have deserved more against the Catalan superstars who killed the contest with a dodgy penalty-kick in the second-half.

However, that did not prevent Brendan Rodgers from beaming brightly as he held aloft his first silverware as Celtic manager while exclaiming excitedly: "I am delighted for the football club. It's about six months and a week since I came in. We talked about what we wanted to achieve and how we wanted to do it. We are certainly well on our way to doing that. I was very pleased with the performance.

"It's something tangible to show for our efforts. Everyone has talked about the great start and the great football, but you want something to show for it. This was out first chance and I felt the players were magnificent. For me, my job is to manage and bring success to Celtic. I am proud to be here as manager and to bring a trophy to the people I love, to the club, to the support and the players.

"It's a huge privilege to be the manager at Celtic and to have the first trophy with my own people is very special. It's a really good feeling and I am delighted for everyone. It's

SCOTT SINCLAIR, who had worked with Brendan Rodgers at Chelsea and Swansea City, joined from Aston Villa on August 6 2016. He scored on his debut as a substitute in the 2-1 win over Hearts at Tynecastle twenty-four hours later.

great for the confidence and sets us up very well. We have a huge job here to sustain this and build on it. But at this moment in time, after six months, it's a great achievement.

"It was an outsanding performance. To play with that level of control and quality in a Cup Final, along with the players' football ideas, was amazing. We scored three good goals and we always looked a threat in the game and, very importantly, the team defended very well, were aggressive and pressed the game at the right moments. Tactically, they played at a high level.

"We have had a lot of games following Champions League matches. Aberdeen had two games in thirty days and obviously had the full week to prepare. But if you look at the intensity and physicality of my team, it really demonstrates how hard and how well they are working on a day-to-day basis and how well they recover in games. What we are trying to achieve is an aggressive way of playing offensively."

Gordon; Lustig, Simunovic, Sviatchenko, Izaguirre; Brown, Armstrong; Roberts (sub: Bitton), Rogic (sub: McGregor), Forrest (sub: Griffiths); Dembele.

League Cup Results

August 10, 2016: Last 16:
CELTIC 5 Rogic (2), Dembele (2,1 pen), Sinclair
MOTHERWELL 0

Gordon; Janko (sub: Ralston), Lustig (sub: McCart), O'Connell, Izaguirre; Brown (sub: Henderson), McGregor; Forrest, Rogic, Sinclair; Dembele.

September 21: Quarter-Final:
CELTIC 2 Forrest, Dembele
ALLOA 0

Gordon; Lustig, Toure, Simunovic (sub: Christie), Tierney; Brown, Armstrong; Roberts (sub: Sinclair), Rogic (sub: Sviatchenko), Forrest; Dembele.

October 23: Semi-Final:
CELTIC 1 Dembele
RANGERS 0

Gordon; Lustig, Simunovic, Sviatchenko, Tierney; Brown, Bitton (sub: Armstrong); Forrest (sub: Gamboa), Rogic (sub: Griffiths), Sinclair; Dembele.

November 27: Final:
CELTIC 3 Rogic, Forrest, Dembele (pen)
ABERDEEN 0

Gordon; Lustig, Simunovic, Sviatchneko, Izaguirre; Brown, Rogic (sub: McGregor); Roberts (sub: Bitton), Armstrong, Forrest (sub: Griffiths); Dembele.

Singing in the Reign

CELTIC 2
ABERDEEN 1
(May 27, 2017)

BRENDAN RODGERS **was standing drenched on the Hampden touchline while his all-conquering players cavorted on the pitch behind him to the strains of "You'll Never Walk Alone".**

A goal deep in stoppage time by Tom Rogic had just beaten Aberdeen to give Celtic the Scottish Cup to complete the historic treble.

Rodgers, in his first season, had led the club to an unprecedented forty-seven game unbeaten sequence against Scottish opposition – something never achieved by any team before his Invincibles.

The TV interviewer stated: "This club have fallen in love with you and you have fallen in love with this club."

The Irishman practically snapped: "No!"

The manager swiftly explained: "I was born into Celtic.

BALANCING ACT...Celtic skipper Scott Brown rests the newly-won Scottish Cup on the head of Kieran Tierney as the champions celebrate completing their historic treble – the first Scottish team ever to go through an entire campaign without defeat in any tournament.

BHOYS ZONE

IVORY COAST midfielder Eboue Kouassi joined Celtic in a £2.8million move from Russian side Krasnodar in January. Moussa Dembele (Fulham), Scott Sinclair (Aston Villa), Cristian Gamboa (West Brom), Dorus de Vries (Nottingham Forest) and Kolo Toure (released by Liverpool) had joined in August.

I was born into a Celtic family. There's been no growing into this club.

"There has only been pride and and it's a huge privilege to manage Celtic. I have always wanted to manage Celtic. I'm here now and I just think it is the right time for everyone, myself and the club."

As the rain still swirled around the national stadium, Rodgers added: "We've created an identity this season and, hopefully, we can build on that and improve over the coming years. What we have achieved has been really spectacular."

Rodgers also described the "special feeling" of emulating Jock Stein and Martin O'Neill after leading Celtic to the fourth treble in their history.

"Maybe the stars were aligned this year," he smiled. " I remember the centenary year for Celtic and there's just a feeling about this season. But don't get me wrong, we've had to earn it. We've worked hard.

"It's a huge honour. I think what the players have achieved and you see how difficult it is, the great history of this club and the great managers and players who have been here before me.

"To have achieved that in the first season, along with everything else that we've done is very humbling.

"I still get a wee bit of a funny feeling, it doesn't sit quite right with me. Jock was a real pioneer in leading the club where they wanted to go. Martin did an incredible job here.

"History will judge me and I've only just begun, so when I leave here people will look at what I did. It's been truly enjoyable. It's a really special feeling today."

A dramatic 2016/17 campaign was edging to a shuddering climax with Celtic and Aberdeen locked at 1-1 in the Scottish Cup Final on a day of crazy changeable weather conditions in Mount Florida on the Saturday afternoon of May 27, 2017.

The champions had been rocked when the Pittodrie outfit had taken the lead through an effort from Jonny Hayes, but, thankfully, Stuart Armstrong had the perfect response with the leveller just over a minute later, a low left-foot drive from the edge of the box that zipped beyond the desperately diving Joe Lewis.

Two minutes into stoppage time, the scoreline hadn't changed – until a moment of magic from the man known as the Wizard of Oz, Tom Rogic. No danger threatened as he picked up a pass from Stuart Armstrong and ambled forward. There was a spurt of acceleration to leave Anthony O'Connor in his slipstream.

Menacingly, Rogic carried into the penalty area, a shimmy one way and then another bamboozled Andy Considine before the Aussie playmaker spotted a space between the keeper and his near post. With a nonchalant sweep of his right foot he tucked the ball sweetly into the net.

About a minute later, referee Bobby Madden blew his whistle for time-up and the Scottish Cup was on its way to the east end of Glasgow to keep the Premiership and the League Cup company in the Celtic Park trophy cabinet.

History had been made with virtually the last kick of the ball.

It had been that kind of season.

Gordon; Lustig, Simunovic, Boyata, Tierney (sub: Rogic); Brown, Armstrong; Roberts (sub: Sviatchenko), McGregor, Sinclair; Griffiths. ■

Scottish Cup

January 22, 2017:
Fourth Round:
ALBION ROVERS 0
CELTIC 3 Sinclair, Dembele, Armstrong

Gordon; Gamboa, Lustig (sub: Simunovic), Boyata, Tierney (sub: McGregor); Brown, Bitton; Forrest (sub: Roberts), Armstrong, Sinclair; Dembele.

February 11:
Fifth Round:
CELTIC 6 Lustig, Dembele (3), Tierney, Brown
INVERNESS CALEY THISTLE 0

Gordon; Lustig, Boyata (sub: Toure), Sviatchenko, Tierney; Brown, Bitton; Forrest, Henderson (sub: McGregor), Sinclair; Dembele (sub: Ciftci).

March 5:
Quarter-Final:
CELTIC 4 Lustig, Dembele (3), Tierney, Brown
ST MIRREN 1 Davis

Gordon; Lustig, Boyata, Sviatchenko, Tierney; Brown, Bitton (sub: Griffiths); Mackay-Steven (sub: Roberts), Armstrong (sub: Kouassi), Sinclair; Dembele.

April 23:
Semi-Final:
CELTIC 2 McGregor, Sinclair (pen)
RANGERS 0

Gordon; Lustig, Simunovic, Boyata, Tierney; Brown, Armstrong; Roberts (sub: Forrest), McGregor (sub: Rogic), Sinclair; Dembele (sub: Griffiths).

May 27:
Final:
CELTIC 2 Armstrong, Rogic
ABERDEEN 1 Hayes

Gordon; Lustig, Simunovic, Boyata, Tierney (sub: Rogic); Brown, Armstrong; Roberts (sub: Sviatchenko), McGregor, Sinclair; Griffiths.

Champions League Results

July 12: 2016   Second Qualifying Round: 1st leg:
LINCOLN RED IMPS 1
CELTIC 0 Casciaro

Gordon; Janko, Ambrose, Sviatchenko, Tierney; Brown, Bitton, Rogic (sub: Armstrong), Christie (sub: Forrest); Dembele (sub: Ciftci), Griffiths.

July 20:   2d leg:
CELTIC 3 Lustig, Griffiths, Roberts
LINCOLN RED IMPS 0 (Aggregate: 3-1)

Gordon; Lustig, Sviatchenko, Tierney (sub: Ajer); Brown, Armstrong; Roberts, McGregor, Forrest; Dembele (sub: Ciftci), Griffiths.

July 27:   Third Qualifying Round: 1st leg:
ASTANA 1 Logvinenko
CELTIC 1 Griffiths

Gordon; Lustig, Ambrose, O'Connell, Tierney; Roberts, Brown, Armstrong (sub: Forrest), McGregor (sub: Rogic); Dembele (sub: Bitton), Griffiths.

August 3:   2nd leg:
CELTIC 2 Griffiths (pen), Dembele (pen)
ASTANA 1 (Aggregate: 3-2) Ibraimi

Gordon; Janko, Lustig, O'Connell, Tierney; Brown, Armstrong (sub: Toure); Roberts (sub: Johansen), McGregor, Forrest (sub: Dembele); Griffiths.

August 17:   Qualifying Play-Off: 1st leg:
CELTIC 5 Rogic, Griffiths (2), Dembele, Brown
HAPOEL BE'ER SHEVA 2 Soares, Melikson

Gordon; Lustig (sub: Janko), Toure, O'Connell, Tierney; Brown, McGregor (sub: Bitton); Forrest, Rogic (sub: Dembele), Sinclair; Griffiths.

August 23:   2nd leg:
HAPOEL BE'ER SHEVA 2 Sahar, Hoban
CELTIC 0 (Aggregate: 5-4)

Gordon; Janko, Lustig, Toure, Tierney; Brown, Bitton; Forrest (sub: Rogic), McGregor (sub: Sviatchenko), Sinclair; Griffiths (sub: Dembele).

GROUP STAGES

September 13: MATCHDAY ONE:
BARCELONA 7 Messi (3), Neymar, Iniesta, Suarez (2)
CELTIC 0

De Vries; Gamboa, Lustig, Toure, Sviatchenko (sub: O'Connell), Tierney; Roberts (sub: Armstrong), Brown, Bitton (sub: McGregor), Sinclair; Dembele.

September 28: MATCHDAY TWO:
CELTIC 3 Dembele (2), Sterling (og)
MANCHESTER CITY 3 Fernandinho, Sterling, Nolito

Gordon; Lustig, Toure, Sviatchenko, Tierney; Brown, Bitton (sub: Griffiths); Forrest (sub: Roberts), Rogic (sub: Armstrong), Sinclair; Dembele.

October 19:   MATCHDAY THREE:
CELTIC 0
BORUSSIA MONCHENGLADBACH 2 Stindl, Hahn

Gordon; Lustig, Toure, Sviatchenko, Tierney; Brown, Bitton (sub: McGregor); Forrest (sub: Roberts), Rogic (sub: Griffiths), Sinclair; Dembele.

November 1:   MATCHDAY FOUR:
BORUSSIA MONCHENGLADBACH 1 Stindl
CELTIC 1 Dembele (pen)

Gordon; Gamboa (sub: Henderson), Lustig, Sviatchenko, Izaguirre; Brown, Armstrong; Forrest (sub: Roberts), Rogic (sub: McGregor), Sinclair; Dembele.

November 23: MATCHDAY FIVE:
CELTIC 0
BARCELONA 2 Messi (2, 1 pen)

Gordon; Lustig, Simunovic, Sviatchenko, Izaguirre; Brown, McGregor (sub: Roberts); Rogic (sub: Bitton), Armstrong, Sinclair (sub: Forrest); Dembele.

December 6:   MATCHDAY SIX:
MANCHESTER CITY 1 Iheanacho
CELTIC 1 Roberts

Gordon; Lustig, Simunovic, Sviatchenko, Izaguirre; Brown, Armstrong; Roberts, Rogic, Forrest (sub: Mackay-Steven); Dembele (sub: Griffiths).

SHOW OF HANDS...Brendan Rodgers leads the applause followed by Gary Mackay-Steven, Anthony Ralston, James Forrest, Scott Sinclair, Callum McGregor and Leigh Griffiths.